REJOICE & BE GLAD

GOSPEL PREACHING
FOR CHRISTIAN FESTIVALS

Also by Scott Cowdell ...

Why Church? Christianity as It Was Meant to Be
(New York: Church Publishing, 2024)

Mimetic Theory and its Shadow: Girard, Milbank, and Ontological Violence
(Studies in Violence, Mimesis, and Culture. East Lansing, MI.:
Michigan State University Press, 2023)

Church Matters: Essays and Addresses on Ecclesial Belonging
(Melbourne: Coventry Press, 2022)

René Girard and the Nonviolent God
(Notre Dame, IN.: The University of Notre Dame Press, 2018)

René Girard and Secular Modernity: Christ, Culture, and Crisis
(Notre Dame, IN.: The University of Notre Dame Press, 2013)

Abiding Faith: Christianity Beyond Certainty, Anxiety, and Violence
(Eugene, OR.: Cascade, 2009; Lutterworth, UK.: James Clark, 2010)

The Ten Commandments and Ethics Today
(Melbourne: Acorn Press, 2008)

God's Next Big Thing: Discovering the Future Church
(Melbourne: John Garratt Publishing, 2004)

A God for This World
(London and New York: Continuum, 2000)

Is Jesus Unique? A Study of Recent Christology
(Theological Inquiries. Mahwah, NJ.: Paulist Press, 1996)

Atheist Priest? Don Cupitt and Christianity
(London: SCM Press, 1988)

In *Rejoice and Be Glad*, theologian Scott Cowdell invites us to consider 18 festivals in the Christian calendar and to ponder their relevance to the world we live in. His sermons contain countless gems of wisdom, wit, scholarship and social commentary. They are a timely reminder of the spiritual, cultural and social value of festivals.

Hugh Mackay AO
Social psychologist and author

A colleague once commented on Scott Cowdell's preaching that 'he spits gold'. I agreed. He uplifts and challenges the people of God. It's rare these days to find homilies like these that build confidence, stretch the mind and deepen faith. Unfailingly centred on Jesus Christ, always via a critical ecclesial lens, here is a feast of creative, tough-minded, Bible-centred sermons that engage our questions, follies and self-deceptions. Readers will indeed rejoice and be glad.

Stephen Pickard
Bishop and Professor of Theology, Canberra

According to Bernard Manning, preaching is a manifestation of the Incarnate Word, from the written word, by the spoken word. It is, therefore, a vocation in its own right. St Paul said, 'Woe to me if I preach not the Gospel'. Some are born preachers, some become preachers and some never do. Perhaps it depends on the fire being ignited. Whether Scott Cowdell was a born preacher I know not but I do know that at some point early in his ministry – I have known him since he was a student – the fire was ignited.

David Richardson AO, OBE
formerly Dean of Adelaide and Melbourne
and the Archbishop of Canterbury's
Representative to the Holy See.

REJOICE & BE GLAD

GOSPEL PREACHING FOR CHRISTIAN FESTIVALS

SCOTT COWDELL

COVENTRY PRESS

Published in Australia by
Coventry Press
33 Scoresby Road
Bayswater VIC 3153

ISBN 9781922589439

Copyright © Scott Cowdell 2024

All rights reserved. Other than for the purposes and subject to the conditions prescribed under the *Copyright Act*, no part of this publication may be reproduced, stored in a retrieval system, or transmitted in any form or by any means, electronic, mechanical, photocopying, recording or otherwise, without the prior permission of the publisher.

Scripture quotations are from the *New Revised Standard Version Bible*, copyright 1989, Division of Christian Education of the National Council of the Churches of Christ in the United States of America. Used by permission. All rights reserved.

Catalogue-in-Publication entry is available from the National Library of Australia
http://catalogue.nla.gov.au

Cover design by Ian James – www.jgd.com.au
Text design by Coventry Press
Cover image Pieter Breughel the Younger (1564-1638)
"Sermon of St John the Baptist" (National Museum in Kraków-MNK)
Set in EB Garamond

Printed in Australia

"... for an obligation is laid on me, and woe to me if I do not proclaim the gospel!"

1 Corinthians 9:16

Contents

Acknowledgments	13
Epiphany	**17**
Epiphany and the Catholic Faith	19
Time to Saddle Up	23
Baptism of the Lord	**27**
The Tsunami and Belief in God	29
The World Begins Again	36
The Presentation of Christ in the Temple (Candlemas)	**41**
Christian Children?	43
Candlemas: Outshining the Power of Death	48
Transfiguration	**53**
Transfigured Desire	55
All in Good Time	61
Passion Sunday (Palm Sunday)	**67**
Topsy Turvy	69
Returning to Our True Country	72
The Darkness of God?	77
Holy Thursday (Maundy Thursday)	**85**
Jesus' Alternative Sacrifice	87
A Tough and Genuine Alternative	91

Good Friday — 95

- Who is the Son of God? — 97
- At-one-ment Beyond Divine Violence — 101
- Good Friday: *Alone in Berlin* — 108

Easter Day (First Sunday of Easter) — 113

- The Resurrection Includes Us — 115
- Caught up in the New Creation — 119
- The Resurrection: But What about the Eggs? — 124

Ascension — 129

- In Heart and Mind there Ascend — 131
- Putting the Powers on Notice — 134
- Caught in the Updraft — 138

Pentecost — 143

- Witness, Weaver and Warrior — 145
- A Blow-up Church? — 150
- Beyond Cynicism, Fatalism and Groupthink — 157

Trinity Sunday — 163

- Good News for Western Culture — 165
- Trinity Starts with Experience — 172
- Growing in the Womb of Love — 176

Corpus Christi — 179

- Beyond Sacrifice and Violence — 181
- Body, Matter, Violence — 185

Mary   **189**

  Something's Missing   191
  Our Long-Lost Half-Sister   194

St Michael and All Angels (Michaelmas)   **199**

  Angels?   201
  All Singing, All Dancing   208

All Saints' Day   **213**

  The Saints: Role Models and More   215
  All Saints' Day, and just in time ...   221

Christ the King (The Reign of Christ)   **225**

  Faith and Relevance   227
  Sovereignty Beyond Monarchy and Republic   230

Christmas (Midnight Mass)   **235**

  What Sort of Lord do we Meet in the Christmas Gospel?   237
  Joyeux Nöel   242

Christmas Day   **247**

  The Word Became Flesh – Yes, *Flesh*   249
  Joy of Heaven to Earth Come Down   254

  Appendix   257

Acknowledgments

- Thanks to Coventry Press and especially to Hugh McGinlay for taking on this project, my second outing with them.

- Thanks to the faith communities in which these sermons were delivered. In most cases these were in the context of longstanding pastoral relationships that I cherished. In the parishes where I have served as an honorary associate priest, I am grateful to the Rectors who (in all but one instance) welcomed my ministry of word and sacrament.

- Thanks to Fr Peter Lindenmayer who set me on the path of "liturgical preaching" and to Canon David Richardson, whose preaching so inspired me – in both cases long ago when I was starting out.

- Thanks to Lisa Carley, too, who heard all of them and kept coming back.

Preface

Two centuries ago, in Jane Austen's time, books of sermons were widely read – especially by ladies of refined sense and sensibility. Such sermons were regarded as wholesome and improving literature. But instead of a genteel pastime I want to offer readers some theological fibre for their spiritual diet and some encouragement for living the Christian life, drawing on the great Christian festivals.

This comes with the reassurance, if any is needed, that liturgical churches and the Christian year they celebrate do not dilute the Gospel with distractions, as some think, but are in fact celebrating the Gospel in all its aspects. The Catholic tradition – inclusively conceived – need not and should not be thought of as Gospel-lite.

The Gospel is most faithfully rendered in harmony. First there is the duet of Good Friday and Easter Day – the systole and diastole of redeemed imaginations and changed lives. Then other voices emerge. There is the strong incarnational theme, associated chiefly with Christmas and with key scenes from Jesus' life according to the Gospels. Then there is a further revealing of who Jesus is at Ascension and of God's nature at Pentecost. This God-for-us, clarified and celebrated on Trinity Sunday, variously constitutes the Church as we see happening with Corpus Christi, Mary and the Saints. All this is Gospel from end to end.

We live at a time of coarsening political discourse and declining public culture, which in America has left a chronically divided nation and a Christian body marked by mutual excommunication. False prophets abound, while self-righteousness thrives on both sides of the culture wars. I lament how identity politics on the left can readily descend into cancel-culture, while Christian nationalism on the right has become Christianly unrecognisable. A candidate at the last election for Governor of Arizona called for a return to "God, Guns and Glory"; what immediately came to my mind was its alliterative antithesis: "Satan, School Shootings and Shame."

Preface

In the midst of all this, the Gospel-formed imagination and the Church that enacts it provides much needed salt and light for the world. Apart from finding a genuine Christian freedom that has escaped self-justifying hostility against the unwelcome other, the major challenges of these times – our climate crisis, the threat of war, racism, new threats to public health, a collapsing social fabric, the worldwide rise of authoritarian populism – will find us unprepared. Hence my modest claim for re-emphasising the Gospel, and my hope that the liturgical Churches will remember this as they celebrate their festivals. These are a treasure in the field, and a pearl of great price. Each festival constitutes an encounter with Christ himself, who is like a diamond that is all-the-more beautiful for its many facets.

Now, a word about the origin and context of these sermons, and a little about this preacher by way of orientation. I am a Research Professor in theology at an Australian university. Since 2004, I have been working with the mimetic theory of René Girard, and this influence will become increasingly evident across the years represented in this collection. Until recently I was the Canon Theologian of my diocese, and a 35-year veteran of the Anglican priesthood. What will also become evident is my strong identification with the Catholic tradition, which is a lifetime preoccupation of mine and has eventually led me (in 2024) to move on from Australian Anglicanism to become a Roman Catholic. In time, I hope to take up my preaching vocation again as a priest in my new Church.

The items selected come from the period 2002-2023 in Canberra, Australia's national capital, nearly all of which were for Eucharistic worship in Anglican parish settings familiar to me. They begin when I was Rector of a major parish (St Paul's, Manuka, 2002-07), later as Honorary Associate priest in a smaller Anglo-Catholic parish, having moved to full-time theological work (All Saints', Ainslie, 2007-18), and most recently in a family-sized congregation, again as an Honorary Associate priest (St Philip's, O'Connor, since 2018). They often comment on current events and use illustrations from film.

Though these sermons span two decades (for each festival I present them in date order), my overarching aims have remained constant. I have always preached the kerygma – the good news of Jesus Christ – avoiding the popular alternative of offering free-floating spiritual advice and mild social concern that does not aim to build up the Church. I always preach gift before task, and task only in the context of gift (Karl Barth's *Gabe und Aufgabe*). I believe that the sermon, like the Gospels, is about Jesus Christ and his inhabiting of the Church, so I employ what might be called a rigorously Christological and a rigorously ecclesial hermeneutic. I also insist on bringing the insights of critical biblical studies and theology to the preaching task. Gospel preaching needs to engage a world of questions, follies and self-deceptions, and must be tough-minded.

I employ the "liturgical preaching" approach, guided by themes proper to the Church's seasons and festivals and using the readings set out thematically in the Common Lectionary. Unlike the newer Revised Common Lectionary, which has congregations reading through Old Testament books, I favour preaching on the coherent combination of Old Testament, Psalm, Epistle and Gospel offered by the Common Lectionary for the "Ordinary Sundays", though both lectionaries usually align for major festivals.

My focus here is on festivals rather than seasons (so no Lent, no Advent). These include Corpus Christi and some Marian feasts that reflect where I was on the Anglican spectrum. My hope is that Roman Catholics, Anglicans/Episcopalians, Protestants in the high-church traditions of Methodism, Lutheranism, and Presbyterianism, and the Orthodox who will forgive my blinkered "Westernism", might all find some encouragement here, along with Evangelicals who have been tempted to "peep over the fence". I hope that all these sisters and brothers in Christ will join me in celebrating the joy of the Gospel that these festivals embody.

Scott Cowdell
Canberra
Birth of St John the Baptist, 24 June 2024

Epiphany

Epiphany and the Catholic Faith

Epiphany, Sunday 6 January 2019,
St Philip's, O'Connor

Isaiah 60:1-6; Psalm 72; Ephesians 3:1-12; Matthew 2:1-12

✝ In the Name of the Father and of the Son and of the Holy Spirit. Amen.

One thing I really value about the Catholic tradition is its comphrehensiveness and its generous openness to the wisdom of the world. It's anything but narrow and suspicious. The Catholic tradition isn't afraid of atheist sceptics like Marx and Freud, for instance. It's critically open to them, and even finds hints of their voices in Scripture and tradition. It isn't afraid of evolutionary biology, even of its radical exponents like Richard Dawkins. Rather, it learns from them, and seeks to understand God creating a world that continues to "create itself" through aeons of natural selection. Neither is it afraid of new thinking on sex and gender, though that one has taken a bit longer. We're finding new insights in the Bible that help us understand Christ as the true liberator of human sexuality. I could go on. There's no truth that human wisdom has devised or uncovered that hasn't been grafted into the Catholic vision in time.

The wise men who come to Jesus in today's gospel – the stargazers, the philosophers, the experts of their day – find in Jesus that their search for truth has moved decisively forward, and that their questioning is taken up into wonder and contemplation. I've long been fascinated by the verse in today's gospel that says of the departing Magi that "they left for their own country by another road". So it is with the Catholic faith. As the wisdom of the ages is brought to Christ, so too the encounter with Christ changes the wisdom of the world; the wise seekers who find Christ return to where they came from by another road. Having encountered Christ and been transformed by him, their view of the world will never be the same. They'll fit their psychology or their biology or their cultural studies or whatever into a bigger framework of meaning than they started with. This is why theology used to be called "the queen of the sciences", because the catholic vision gathers together *but also illuminates* all truth, at its best leaving out nothing.

Another thing I like about the Catholic vision, along with its comprehensiveness, is its confidence, its boldness, because these days we need to be recovering some confidence and boldness in a Church that too often lacks it. Epiphany is a story to build this confidence and boldness, because it puts the bullies on notice. Which bullies? Well, first there's Herod, who I like to imagine being played by Kevin Spacey, as in *House of Cards*. With delicious irony, Matthew arranges things so that the powers that be, the future enemies of Jesus, Herod and his cronies, are informed in no uncertain terms who the *real* King is. And it's not just Herod. The wise men are in fact Persian wise men, and of course Persia, or Babylon, was the place where God's people were exiled. Is Matthew telling us that the top echelon among Israel's former enemies is now lining up to do homage?

This idea is certainly there in today's Old Testament reading, from Isaiah, which Matthew would have meditated on when thinking out his gospel narrative. Isaiah invites God's people to take courage. Once they were a beaten, exiled people, but one day even Kings will come to the brightness of their rising, and the foreigners who once enslaved them will come with gifts to honour them. From Midian, Ephah and Sheba they'll come, to offer gold for a king, and incense for a God. You can see where Matthew got his inspiration – the Magi are given to us by Matthew to illustrate how God has decisively turned the tables, how the day of God's favour has dawned. Matthew might be telling us that even former conquerors are now turning up, but with the boot firmly on the other foot.

What's more, the bullies aren't just earthly ones. They're heavenly ones as well. And here we can understand the real purpose of that perplexing star in today's gospel. We don't have to read Epiphany as a story about an actual star, and then wonder how a star can stop over a house. We don't have to scour ancient history and do computer back-projections of comet movements to uncover what might actually have happened, as some well-meaning but wrongheaded scientists have tried to do – as if the point of this gospel is dependent on astronomy. No, Matthew uses astronomy to point to theology, or more correctly he uses *astrology* to point to theology. Stars in the ancient world weren't just giant thermo-nuclear furnaces, as we now know them to be. Rather, they were more astrological than astronomical. The stars were understood to be powerful, semi-divine beings. In many cultures, they were personified as we see in the naming of constellations, and they were worshipped. The half-hearted faith of some today in their horoscopes – that their future is revealed in the stars – is an echo of astrological beliefs that held great sway in the ancient world.

But biblical faith from the beginning has told a different story. The God of the Bible, right at the start of Genesis, creates the two great lights – the sun and the moon. This isn't a Sunday School version of stellar evolution, which we have to take literally. Rather, it's a statement of faith about what sort of world we now live in, and what sort of confidence we can have. The creation narrative in Genesis robs the cosmic powers of their hold over people's lives – if the God of the Israelites has created them, then they can't be worshipped and they shouldn't be feared. And so it is in today's gospel. The star is a symbol of all the heavenly powers, all the unseen forces that ancient people took so seriously. Thus a cosmic terror is muzzled, and it submits to Jesus Christ. It has met its match!

Elsewhere in the gospels, we see this same use of mythological imagery as it's ripped from its ancient pagan context and redeployed to illustrate real-world truths of actual history – truths confirmed in Jesus' day and in our day. These are truths that the first Christians knew, and that we still know, about Jesus having the power to change hearts and imaginations, to change lives and destinies. So, for example, when a fish from the ocean deeps brings up a coin for Jesus to give to Peter for the temple tax (Matthew 17:24-27) – up from the mythical realm of chaos, that is – that realm of chaos is being put in its place, just as at the start of Genesis, while at the same time the sacrificial religio-cultural system of the Temple that demands the tax is being gently mocked. Likewise, when the storms are stilled on the lake, or when the sun is darkened at noon, or when the demons are driven out and the dead are raised, we're given symbolic reassurance that all the little-understood forces that so ruled and circumscribed the lives of ancient peoples are now firmly on notice. There's a new kid on the block! His name is Jesus Christ! He is now the force to be reckoned with.

So, friends, we take heart – in our lives, in our Church, in our world, *certainly* in the face of our doubts and our confusions. We have found our way to where the answers lie, we can recover our confidence, we can risk the adventure of faith. Nothing in this complex, wonderful, occasionally terrible world need stop us – no earthly power, no toxic spiritual something-or-other. Today, in this Epiphany Eucharist, we celebrate Christ as the meeting point of all truth, and as our starting point, once again, for the adventure of living the Catholic faith.

The Lord be with you...

Time to Saddle Up

Epiphany, Sunday 8 January 2023,
St Philip's, O'Connor

Isaiah 60:1-6; Psalm 72:1-7, 10-14; Ephesians 3:1-12; Matthew 2:1-12

☩ In the Name of the Father and of the Son and of the Holy Spirit. Amen.

I've talked to you before about visiting Auschwitz, in Poland, and the death cell of Fr Maximillian Kolbe, the Franciscan who voluntarily took the place of a Jewish prisoner slated for execution. Many Christians like him refused Nazism's powers and principalities at the cost of their lives. In Berlin, we visited the Catholic memorial Church in Charlottenberg, Mary Queen of Martyrs, honouring all the Christians who died resisting the Nazis. It's a brutalist concrete architectural masterpiece, with a profoundly moving story to tell about God's power over transcendent brutality. This is nothing other than the self-giving love of Jesus Christ – an unlikely power, showing up how weak the world's powers and principalities actually are. I've told you before, too, about the Carmelite convent at Dachau, outside Munich, which you enter through the camp's back wall. It's called the Carmel of the Holy Blood. Its community of nuns gives perpetual witness to where world-transforming power really lies, in a place where many others concluded that God must be dead.

All of these take up the witness of St Paul, testified to in our Ephesians reading this morning: "to make everyone see what is the plan of the mystery hidden for ages in God who created all things, so that through the church the wisdom of God in its rich variety might now be made known to the rulers and powers in the heavenly places". And suffering for this witness, Paul in today's epistle tells his supporters not to worry, because this is the Church's glory: its costly witness in defence of the downtrodden, and especially its martyrs who proclaim God's abundant life.

Yet the Church doesn't always give this clear witness, does it? This struck me at the Holocaust Memorial in Lyon. The Catholic Church in Vichy France had not, by and large, stood up to the Nazis, with many Christians in favour of deporting the Jews. Among those killed for their resistance, though, I did note the name of one Dominican priest. I prayed that if I ever faced such a challenge, I'd have the faith and courage to do what he did. But so many Christians just play along, don't they, with no clear appreciation of what faith entails – from today's godless religious leadership in Russia, for instance, to the Bible thumping far-right fanatics in America's new if stillborn House of Representatives?

Friends, our Old Testament readings today paint a picture of God coming to rescue and deliver God's beloved people from hostile powers, at a time when powers in the heavens and powers of the nations were not readily distinguished. And from this Old Testament picture of kings coming to do homage, bringing gold and frankincense, comes Matthew's story of Jesus' Epiphany in today's gospel – though Matthew adds one more gift: there's not just gold for a king and incense for a God; there's also myrrh for anointing the dead, because Jesus' power over evil is most clearly revealed in his profoundly symbolic death.

Today's Gospel pits Jesus against Herod, who ends up blindsided and powerless. The stargazers and pundits of the day are drawn to Jesus, before whom all the powers, heavenly and earthly, bow down. According to this imaginative vision of Matthew, Herod and all the bullies like him, then and now, have met their match. They can do their worst, as the martyrs testify, because the threat of suffering and death has been overcome by a greater power.

This power is at work when Baptism and Eucharist take hold of lives, calling us to a larger identity, to a more profound existence, to a domestic heroism unimagined by the horde of drones and patsies who prop up today's powers and principalities. God has a higher purpose for us than that, and the star of Epiphany points our way to it. All the cosmic powers align in homage to Jesus Christ – an image of the human condition and of human history coming right at last.

Here today, friends, you and I enact this reality in word and sacrament, we dive into it. That way, when we leave here we can do so with a new sense of anticipation. Epiphany reminds us that there's more on offer here, and more at stake, than many have bargained for. Epiphany reassures us, and it calls us to saddle up.

The Lord be with you ...

Baptism of the Lord

The Tsunami and Belief in God

Baptism of the Lord, Sunday 9 January 2005, Year A,
St Paul's Manuka

Isaiah 42:1-9; Psalm 29; Acts 10:34-43; Matthew 3:13-17

† In the Name of the Father and of the Son and of the Holy Spirit. Amen.

How can we continue to believe in God in the light of those appalling television images of recent weeks from around the Indian Ocean? The waves themselves, captured on camcorders in the hands of happy holidaymakers suddenly confronted by something unimaginable; the chaos surging down on people out of a clear blue sky, sweeping tens of thousands to their deaths and others to safety with a randomness that mocks our careful plans, our reasonable expectations, and the illusion that we're in control of things. And then images of the aftereffects, with blighted landscapes, abandoned towns, mass graves, and always the bereaved – the struggling, the searching, the sobbing. How can we believe in God in the light of all this?

If believing in God means believing that all will go well and predictably for us in life, that sickness and disaster can be kept at bay, that happiness and well-being are our inheritance by right as children of a benevolent God, then the Boxing Day earthquake and its resultant tsunamis spell an end to belief in God. Let's just admit this and move on. Perhaps we in the West have become too spoiled by our many successes – in husbanding the forces of nature, in curing diseases, in achieving a high level of technological mastery and economic wellbeing – that we can deny the universal human realities of failure, disappointment and suffering, and keep believing in a Father Christmas god well into adulthood. But the tough reality of life in this world, the only world we know, eventually breaks through for many naïve believers and the benighted faith of childhood is knocked over.

This should not surprise us or alarm us. The death of God being announced by letter writers to our newspapers in recent weeks can actually mark the first step toward a mature and realistic faith, so that belief in the real God, and mature faith, only comes when the Father Christmas god finally collapses under the weight of his own unlikelihood in the face of life's bitter realities. The path to mature belief, then, is often through the fires of doubt, darkness and atheism. Many of you will know that what I'm saying is true from your own experience of learning to do it tough with the real God in the real world.

So, if we're to believe in God, our belief has to be big enough to cope with earthquakes and tsunamis on the world scale, along with depression and conflict, with failure and chronic illness in our own lives. Our belief has to be big enough to stare into the heart of darkness that we humans make for ourselves, too, so we're not forced – like Franz Rosenzweig, a Jewish theologian – to admit in despair that the God of Israel's covenant must have died in Auschwitz.

Our belief in God has to be big enough for us to keep faith when our own life is unravelling and ending, and when the brute natural forces that made the world of which we're a part churn up that world on the way to some new beginning of life. Our belief in God has to be big enough for us when the discoveries of modern science and history and psychology show-up the storybook faith of childhood as painfully inadequate to the facts. Again, the path of faith in the living God is a challenging, maturing path, far more demanding than gentle Jesus meek and mild and a home for all good children beyond the bright blue sky.

The temptation for many people of faith, though, is to soften this harsh and confronting reality – of not knowing and not understanding yet believing and hoping nonetheless – by trying to make sense of it all, all the suffering and blighted hopes, trying to make it better, trying to draw the sting... "Don't worry, God has a purpose for it all – it's God's will".

Someone has called this the "Godswill" argument, because it really is swill! The Bible at its best never tries to make sense of human suffering and natural travail in this way, as if a neat theory is faith's answer for humanity *in extremis*. The Bible leaves that slick alternative to real faith to the likes of the false prophets, and to Job's comforters, who're sure they can see a purpose in Job's suffering. I prefer the Bible, I prefer Job, and I prefer the Psalmists, who lamented honestly, who refused to sing happy songs in the face of tragedy, and yet who knew that God remained a reliable reality despite it all.

The faith of the Bible is a paradoxical faith that can hold together the fact of suffering and the fact of God's love without seeking to resolve that paradox – not seeking to resolve it into atheism, on the one hand, which surrenders belief in God or, on the other hand, seeking to resolve the paradox into a naïve faith that denies the real fact of suffering. Mature Christian faith, biblical faith, holds both together. It doesn't seek a theoretical answer. It doesn't identify God with neatness, with closure, with resolution. Faith like that has been called "Cosmic Toryism", always intent on drawing a veil of purpose over the ill-fitting facts of life. Mature faith, however, beckons us from the other side of atheism, when such false assurances have ceased to convince us. Mature faith can live with the paradox of a loving God in a suffering world, without being scandalised.

So, there's little I can offer you today by way of theoretical assurance. Of course, I came to see from my scientific training as a young man that the world is a deeply interconnected web of cause and effect, of great age, and that we humans evolved at the end of an incomprehensibly long struggle of life, which itself only became possible after even longer aeons of geological and meteorological upheaval. We humans wouldn't have emerged as a species if a giant asteroid impact hadn't cleared the dinosaurs out of the way so we mammals could inherit the earth. And we wouldn't have spread over the earth and diversified without tectonic plates shifting to create new continents in the same way the Indian plate moved to cause the Boxing Day earthquake.

Our earth fumed and seethed and broke open and erupted long before the emergence of life until eventually the conditions were right, and once life emerged, an impossibly long, impossibly violent and bloody process of evolution was necessary to produce us, with over 96% of all species that ever lived becoming extinct along the way as the necessary price for our being here. We are the product, friends, of the very natural processes that produced the disaster of Boxing Day. And so, if God is to be believed in as our creator, it's through the processes of *this* world, the only world we know, that God created and continues to create life.

Perhaps things could have been different, but if the process was different, if the world was different, then it's unlikely we human beings would have emerged from it. As the mid-twentieth century Oxford theologian Austin Farrer succinctly put it, "we could only wish the world to be made otherwise, if we could wish to be creatures of another sort".[1] These considerations bring the paradox of faith into greater relief – it seems that this is the way the world has to be for human life to take shape on it, let alone for human life to demonstrate its true greatness by rising to the many challenges of an imperfect world.

But while I recognise that God has created this sort of world, and that a different, perhaps safer world would hardly likely be a world able to produce human beings, I must still admit that none of this amounts to a neat and definite piece of reassurance in the face of suffering. Even with these insights of modern science in view, the fact of suffering still remains a great burden to the human heart, defying resolution at the level of theory.

---

1   Austin Farrer, *A Science of God* (London: Geoffrey Bles, 1966), 61.

But if belief in God is a paradox that lives with the fact of suffering, if this is biblical faith, then is there any good news in the Bible to help us get hold of this faith, to make our way in this sort of world, to live with this paradox? Yes, I think that there is. And on this feast day of the Baptism of Jesus, I believe we're in a good place to see just what this good news at the heart of our faith really is.

The Baptism of Jesus by John the Baptist, at the heart of our celebration today, is a highly symbolic story. It's a reminder that God conquers our fear and gives us the confidence to live bravely. At its heart is the imagery of water, and how timely this is for our purposes in the light of the recent disaster. Water was the chaotic, terrifying element *par excellence* in the imaginatively, symbolically rich dreamtime stories of the Bible – water covered a dark and formless earth before God's act of creation, water reclaimed the earth in the story of Noah and the great flood, and water threatened Israel in its flight from slavery in Egypt at the Red Sea.

It was over the waters, over this chaotic element of biblical faith, that the Spirit of God moved in the Genesis creation myth to bring an ordered world from chaos. And in the same way it was this chaotic element of water that God vowed never to call forth again as an instrument of judgment, in God's covenant with Noah, setting up the rainbow as a sign – a rainbow that isn't perhaps visible from the Chapter House of St Andrew's Cathedral in Sydney, with talk from there this week of a new flood sent in judgment from God. Again, it's this chaotic element of water that's symbolically defeated in our Psalm today – perhaps the oldest in the Psalter, and based we're told on a hymn to an ancient storm God, but now made the servant of Yahweh and put very firmly in his place. Hence, we read in our Psalm today that the God of the Bible is seen enthroned on the water flood, as King forever.

In other words, the good news of this God is for hope beyond all the chaos of life and history, symbolised so often in the Bible by water. Hence even the threatened coastlands can look up in hope for the revealing of God's new law of things, as Isaiah joyfully expresses it in our Old Testament reading today.

All this imagery points to the meaning of water as it appears in today's Gospel of Jesus' baptism. Into this symbolic element of chaos Jesus descends, to be raised up symbolically from death to life in his baptism. The Spirit that alights on him in today's Gospel, like a dove, recalls Noah's dove, who has ranged over a world of chaos and conflict to seek a place where human beings might at last find rest, refreshment, peace and hope. And the dove has at last found that place in Jesus Christ. As God creates order from chaos in the first creation, so in Jesus at his baptism the symbolism testifies to a new creation, to a new world for human beings, to a new home and a new future for human beings in Jesus Christ. He is the key to understanding God's purposes, according to our Acts reading today, according to our creed, according to the Eucharist we celebrate, and according to all our best instincts as Christian disciples.

God, and faith in God, and belief in God for Christians, with all the paradoxical reality of suffering taken into account, can only be a belief in the God of Jesus Christ. Only with Jesus is the fact of suffering admitted yet transcended. Only in Jesus Christ is the human struggle taken fully seriously by God, with all the threat, all the hurt, all the uncertainty of human life shouldered by God personally – *and all the blame*! When we talk about Jesus as divine and human, we imagine a humanity that can live in a cruel and chaotic world and yet know it as God's world and as our world; when we talk about Jesus as divine and human, we imagine a God who is anything but theoretically remote from real life, a God who bears the burden of creation from within it, who shares the travail of human life. In his baptism, in the wilderness temptations immediately following after, throughout his ministry and in the travail of his death, Jesus is God with us, drinking the cup of human life and suffering to its dregs.

This is the Christian answer to atheism, then: not a neat theory or a slick theological answer; not the denial of suffering; nothing to do with closure, certainty or anything else that's unequal to the often harsh and ill-fitting facts of life. But simply Jesus himself, and the Spirit that makes him real among us, and our own lives as his disciples, and the counter-cultural fact of our life together as Church across every barrier of human exclusion and hostility. Here is our answer to the challenge to faith of disaster and suffering and the apparent Godlessness of the world. Jesus is the answer, his cross is the answer, his sacramental presence in the thick of it is the answer – and you're the answer, I'm the answer, called to be living signs of hope, bearing the paradox of a loving God in the uncertain, sometimes horrible world of which we're a part.

The Lord be with you...

The World Begins Again

Baptism of the Lord, 8 January 2006, Year B,
St Paul's, Manuka

Genesis 1:1-5; Psalm 29; Acts 19:1-7; Mark 1:4-11

✝ In the Name of the Father and of the Son and of the Holy Spirit. Amen.

Something I enjoyed reading over the break was my friend Tom Frame's new biography of Harold Holt – the Prime Minister who bridged the old and the new Australia. But more than anything Holt achieved politically, what people remember most was the manner of his death. Tragically lost off Portsea in 1967, Holt's death quickly achieved mythic proportions, with various conspiracy theories and tales spun around the plain facts of a drowning.

Something similar happened with the baptism of Jesus. The plain facts were probably these: Jesus was a young spiritual seeker, on the cusp of discerning his extraordinary vocation from the God of Israel, who gravitated for a time to John the Baptist and his radical movement, before moving on to something more inclusive, more joyful, as he came more into his own.

We know that John the Baptist had a strong following in those days, which we see reflected in our Acts reading today, with a group of people who had only known John's Baptism, and who were subsequently baptised in the name of Jesus. Indeed, a religion of John the Baptist worshippers can still be found today, called the Mandaeans. And another thing. It seems clear that by coming for John's baptism of repentance, Jesus was identifying with the rest of sinful humanity in its hunger for God's grace. Whatever Jesus' special closeness to God meant, whatever Jesus' sinlessness meant, it certainly didn't mean remoteness from the whole complex and compromised human struggle.

These were the facts, then, and the Gospels have significantly reworked and elaborated them. First of all, we know that the Gospel writers all make a point of subordinating John the Baptist to Jesus at every turn – Jesus is *numero uno*; the Baptist is *numero due*! So, in Luke we have two annunciations, to Mary and to Elizabeth; we have two births, with no doubt about who got top billing, and we have that marvellous scene where the foetal John the Baptist leaps in the womb to greet the foetal Jesus. In the fourth Gospel, John the Baptist plainly confesses that he's not the Messiah, but only the one preparing the way of the Lord; he says of Jesus 'I must decrease that he may increase'. And in Mark today, the Baptist tells the world that he's only the supporting act, giving Jesus top billing. Clearly, the Gospel writers want to put straight any remaining followers of John the Baptist, leaving them in no doubt that they've backed the wrong horse.

But the elaborating doesn't finish there. The baptism of Jesus is presented as a profoundly symbolic, profoundly mystical beginning for the whole world. It's not just any baptism, with a digital camera and an indulgent uncle. This is nothing less than the creation of the world beginning over again. And thanks to the lectionary today we have other readings to help us see the point.

We have the myth of creation from Genesis 1, with God's spirit moving on the face of the deep to create the world. And we have a like-minded Psalmist celebrating the creative power of Israel's God – with God's voice thundering upon the great waters; with God enthroned above the water-flood. This is the imaginative backdrop that today's Gospel gives us for the Baptism of Jesus. Here the Spirit of God moves again upon the waters, the voice of the Lord thunders out again: "*this* is my beloved son" – Jesus as God's new creation, Jesus as God's new beginning for the world God loves. This is the message we're meant to take from Jesus' baptism loud and clear.

Now, what might this mythically charged spiritual conviction mean for you and for me? It helps if we understand the threatening nature of water and flood and chaos in ancient near-eastern mythology. These all represented the dark side of the force – they were sacred, and they were dangerous. They were understood as the opposite of the stable, reliable, safe world of dry land – they were the menacing "other" that threatened the reassuringly familiar. They're like other sacred dualisms we see in today's readings: light versus dark, for instance, mountains like Lebanon and Sirion verses deserts like Kadesh, and forests, too, as the dark obverse of the safer, open world people preferred to live in.

Here are all the spiritually-charged features of life in a pre-modern world – a world of wood-nymphs in forests, of trolls lurking in Halls of Mountain Kings in wait for an unwary Peer Gynt, of water sprites and sea monsters, and everything else that goes bump in the night of folk imagination. And what is the Bible's answer? It's to imagine a high God above all this, unfazed by the paralysing chaos of the oceans, or that other chaotic realm, the whirling, shifting desert, not overawed by the remote and towering mountains or the dark, impenetrable forests, but a God before whom all these mythically charged realities become just nature, just phenomena, just stuff. Instead of a sacred cosmos, then, we find ourselves well on the way to a natural world and to the practice of science – a world we can farm and investigate and appreciate, not a world we have to fear, full of capricious sacred forces that need pacifying.

Thus, the Bible begins demythologising the sacred cosmos, laying the foundations of today's secular world, our world, which we can shape and make our own. And the religion of this God, the God of Israel, the great lover and liberator, the God of history and human thriving is a religion beyond dualism – beyond a fundamentally divided and hostile world. It's a religion of one world, of nations as friends not entrenched enemies, of human beings who don't read their world dualistically, who don't think all the time of us and them, of me and mine under constant threat. A world made for peace is the creation of our God, and lives made for poised, non-anxious self-confidence and hence fit for healthy relationships.

Jesus sets the example by standing with sinners at his baptism, demonstrating that holiness is not about purity but about loving, compassionate solidarity; that our God does not sponsor a world where those close to God can and should look down on others, or keep them at arm's length. Jesus never did this in his extraordinary ministry. From beginning to end, he sought out the lost sheep of the house of Israel, and his was a holiness that was obviously not off-putting to the prostitutes and tax collectors and others whose lives were lived on the underside of polite society. Jesus knew no such sacred distinctions, which perpetuated all the other dualisms of a pre-biblical cosmic vision. Jesus knew one world, one humanity, and was sure enough in his God to believe that way and live that way.

And so can we. This is the new world our God creates in the baptism of Jesus, inviting us to take our part in it. Our Acts reading today tells us of some of our early ancestors in the faith, in the Ephesian Church, who are baptised in Jesus' name. His life of freedom in the Spirit immediately became their life, just as it did for us in our baptism. All this has been done for us. The power of the new creation has claimed us in our baptism and now comes alive for us today in word and sacrament. It's up to us now to go from here and be a Church that believes it, a Church beyond fear of the other, beyond the nervous self-justifying anxiety that makes the world go around. None of this for us – we know who we are. We're baptised newborns in a new creation, which God liberates humanity to enjoy.

Myths around the death of Harold Holt show what a symbolically and historically significant event it was. So too with the baptism of Jesus. For us it points to the most significant thing of all: that God is making a new world in Jesus Christ, and that this new world is our home, our birthright in baptism, our gift to renew week by week at the Eucharist, our inheritance day by day in the liberating habit of prayer, and our challenge to live out before a world that prefers its fears, its dualisms and its entrenched hostilities.

The Lord be with you...

The Presentation of Christ in the Temple (Candlemas)

Christian Children?

Presentation of Christ in the Temple, 4 February 2018,
St Philip's, O'Connor

Malachi 3:1-4; Psalm 84; Hebrews 2:14-18; Luke 2:22-40

☦ In the Name of the Father and of the Son and of the Holy Spirit. Amen.

The Presentation of Christ in the Temple is a festival of light, hence its traditional name of Candlemas. Christ is the light of the world – revealed to the Gentiles yet also the glory of his own people Israel. The Eastern Orthodox, who love the symbolism of light and who make Epiphany into a second Christmas, were very big on this festival from early on, and later it caught on in Western Catholicism. Even that Protestant, Cranmer, put it into the first Anglican prayer books. Christ the light of the world is a comforting, welcome light but also a disturbing, exposing one. He is a beacon and a lighthouse that guides and reassures us, but also a searchlight or a floodlight that seeks out and reveals what's hidden. His light is both revelation and judgment – he shows up the darkness of our hearts at the same time as he reveals God's love and God's will for us.

These two dimensions are there in our Malachi reading today, and in our Gospel. The Lord who comes to his temple is like a refiner's fire and like laundry soap, to clarify and purify the people of God. While in the gospel the aged Simeon in the temple warns Mary that Jesus will be a sign for the fall as well as the rising of many in Israel; and that she will not have an easy time of it as the mother of this Jesus, with a sword piercing her own heart.

So, friends, Jesus is both good news and bad news, as the old joke says: good news of God's love and God's liberating, transforming claim on our lives; but bad news for our follies and our pretensions, for our pride and our self-delusion. He loves us so much that he wants to free us from our worst selves and to change us – and, of course, many find that prospect unwelcome and uncomfortable. But the letter to the Hebrews today reminds us that the love of God is at work freeing us from our sins and our burdens *from the inside* – not over an impossible distance but from *within* the human experience, from *within* the ongoing story of God's people. Jesus is one of us, and because he's one of us, he can help us undergo the challenges that all human beings face in general, and that people of faith face in particular. God is revealed and grows among us, to transform a much-loved people from the inside, up close and personal.

And now I want to talk *about* our children, and I want to speak *to* our children, because today's gospel is one of the few gospel readings referring to Jesus as a child. There's the infant Jesus and, at the end, there's the mention of Jesus' childhood in Nazareth, growing in strength and wisdom. This is particularly appropriate because today the parish marks the beginning of a new school year for its children. If Jesus' journey towards his destiny began in the temple, so children today begin the journey towards their destiny when their parents present them at the school gate.

I have an old black and white photo of me, aged 5, in my brand-new school uniform in our Brisbane back yard, with its rickety old fence and its banana trees, ready for my first day at Geebung Primary School. I look surprisingly confident, which is strange because apparently, I found the transition to school quite traumatic, just as I later found the transition from primary school to high school to be, and again from school to university. Anyway, my grandfather was there to wave me off and I'm told that he turned to my mother and said, "Well, he's off to work", meaning that my journey towards adult life and responsibility and independence had begun.

The Presentation of Christ in the Temple (Candlemas)

For our children, following Jesus as they grow up, the journey of life is meant to lead them into strength and wisdom, as it led Jesus. But for our children, this journey towards strength and wisdom takes place in the company of Jesus, so that he can be their role model – as Christian children, they grow up as friends and admirers of the child Jesus. This means that they must learn to know Jesus, to pray to him, to be familiar with his story in the Gospels, to serve him in the small actions and in the big decisions of their young lives, to worship him faithfully and regularly, and to try to be like him. And all of this they will need to do in a world that tells them constantly to forget about Jesus and live just as they like.

But Jesus has put his mark on us in our baptism, with that cross on our forehead – our first tattoo, even if it's not visible. We do well to remember that it's there; we do well to remember that, before we could respond and do anything either right or wrong, Jesus claimed us in love to be his own forever. So while we grow up as children and teenagers into young adulthood and beyond, we can know that Jesus walked the same road, that Jesus had to learn and make mistakes like we do, that Jesus had to learn to get on with people, and had to suffer the fears and upsets of childhood, while he grew in strength and wisdom in God's friendship.

This may all sound strange and old-fashioned in an age when children are spoiled and indulged and seldom held accountable; when many children slavishly copy their peers, while ignoring their parents and scarcely registering the existence let alone the claim of others, entrusting their imaginations to wireless devices that are never out of their hands. For Christian children, however, following Jesus as they grow up, God's call for them to become strong and wise is a call to out-grow being infantile, selfish, thoughtless and unfeeling, barely aware of others, and forgetful of God.

As a boy, I loved being an altar server and worshipping God in the Eucharist. I believe that God claimed my life to be his witness as a boy, calling me to the priesthood around the time of my confirmation at age 11. Today's Psalm is one I loved as a boy:

"How lovely is your dwelling place, O Lord God of hosts; my soul has a desire and longing to enter the courts of the Lord; my heart and my flesh rejoice in the living God". Later, when I was ordained as a priest in my late-20s, I had some words from this Psalm on my prayer card, summing up the meaning of my life: "The sparrow has found her a home and the swallow a nest where she may lay her young; even your altar, O Lord of hosts, my king and my God".

So to children I say that God is calling you to know and to love him, and to become like Jesus, and to take your place among God's people for the rest of your life, and not to give up when other teenagers stop going to church and you may not feel like going any more, and you badger your parents until they let you stay home. God had his hooks into Jesus, and into me, from a very young age, and children should expect that God will be pressing his claim on them, too, even from a young age.

The parents of Jesus had to get used to this idea, which no doubt came as a bit of shock. The older generation was wiser and more discerning, perhaps; with the wisdom of years and the long practice of faith, Simeon and Anna saw further. Christian children need the faith of their parents to guide them, to be open to the surprises that God might have in store for them, and to respect the claim of God on their children's lives. Our children also need the example and the discernment of the next generation up if they're to be strengthened in their life with God, just as the older generation need the hope and confidence that seeing faith take root in a new generation can bring.

In all these ways, the faith of Jesus himself, strengthened by and in turn strengthening the faith of Joseph and Mary, of Simeon and Anna, is a faith that will take root in our children, so that in time the world will see in them the fulfilment of God's promises. Should we expect anything less from God, and from our children and grandchildren, than this?

The Presentation of Christ in the Temple (Candlemas)

Let us pray.

☩ *Lord, now you let your servant go in peace. Your word has been fulfilled. For my eyes have seen the salvation which you have prepared in the sight of every people. A light to lighten the gentiles, and the glory of your people Israel.*

Candlemas: Outshining the Power of Death

Presentation of Christ in the Temple, 3 February 2019,
St Philip's, O'Connor

Malachi 3:1-4; Psalm 84; Hebrews 2:14-18; Luke 2:22-40

✝ In the Name of the Father and of the Son and of the Holy Spirit. Amen.

Over the last five weeks we've seen the Christmas season expand into the Epiphany season, with each week bringing a new revealing of Christ and his universal mission. Today we celebrate his Presentation as an infant in the Temple, as we move towards the climax of these Epiphany stories with the Transfiguration. An old name for the Presentation is Candlemas, with its focus on the light of Christ through the use of candles. In France, it's called Chandeleur, as in chandelier or candelabra, when the French eat crepes – which are round as a reminder of the sun's disk.

Now, this is all very interesting, but what does it have to do with our lives in the real world? The first hint comes at Christmas, when we hear from Isaiah that "on those living in the land of the shadow of death, light has dawned" and from Luke that the Christ child comes "to shine on those who live in darkness, and in the shadow of death". In today's gospel, in his account of the Presentation, Luke further weaves this conviction into the story of Jesus' origins. We're introduced to two ancient prophets of Israel, Simeon and Anna, who are both clearly living in the land of death's shadow due to their advanced age.

Both of them give way to long, pent-up rejoicing at the sight of Jesus. Here is the long-expected hope of Israel and Judah,

The Presentation of Christ in the Temple (Candlemas)

the Messiah anticipated by Malachi at the very end of the Old Testament, from whom we hear this morning, whose arrival is celebrated by Simeon and Anna on behalf of God's ancient people.

For Simeon, it means a release at last from his long vigil: his cry "Lord, now you are dismissing your servant in peace" is the same phrase that a slave would use in the formal action of being released from his servitude by the master. At last, Simeon can close his tired old eyes, and meet his death in peace, because of what he's been privileged to witness. As for old Anna, a widow of nearly seven decades standing, she forgets her status as a woman and her likely shame as a cursed and marginal figure and rejoices openly, probably startling the passers-by with her zeal for the infant Jesus. His light has banished the darkness of death, bringing a new dawn for Israel and for all humanity.

Friends, this theme of death is taken up in our Epistle today from Hebrews, and how Jesus comes among us to end humanity's enslavement to death's power. There's that slavery motif again, which we hear on the lips of old Simeon in the act of casting it off. Let me talk to you about this power of death, which Hebrews associates with the power of the Devil. But let's make sure that we don't get tangled up.

We're not talking here about death as a natural biological process, which entered the evolutionary journey of life on earth as a by-product of sexual reproduction, as we now know to be the case. That is, when evolution gave rise to new forms of life with cells kept genetically pristine for reproduction, all the other body cells could then specialise into a diversity of new organs and functions. But the result of all the fashioning and refashioning of new types of body parts led to all those non-reproductive cells losing genetic coherence over time, which is the reason why our bodies age, decay and die.

My apologies for this compressed lesson in evolutionary biology, but my point in giving it is that biological death is now seen to be the price that complex sexually reproducing lifeforms pay for all their rich diversity, not to mention all that sex! So, ageing and death, the mere fact of death, is biological, and it's ultimately unavoidable – it's the price we pay for being the wonderful creatures that we are. But the power of death and the fear of death are cultural, and these are things that we *can* do something about.

Now, of course, a lot of people will tell you that they don't fear death. And that's certainly true. I've seldom if ever had a pastoral conversation with someone in their mid-90s who isn't tired of the long burden of years and who isn't ready to relax into the gentle embrace of death. They feel they've lived long enough. Likewise, I've talked with younger, terminally ill people who are at peace with their coming death. And with military people on the eve of deployment who are philosophical about their very real risk of death. But I think that the power of death and the fear of death work more subtly.

For some, the power of death and the fear of death is a fear of being forgotten, of death revealing that their lives didn't amount to much. Hence for them the power of death is the power to unravel the identity they've built up. Here the Devil is best understood as representing the voice of accusation, because Satan in the Bible is always ultimately the accuser, the prosecutor, telling us that we're unworthy, that we're unloved and unlovable, that we're unemployable, unmarriageable, and failures at the things we've set out to achieve. And so, our death looms not as a natural biological process – as the ending that gives our life some shape and opens the way for new generations. Instead, our death looms as a threat to who we think we are, as an acid that eats away at the narrative continuity of our life story.

I think that this is why many people today are so keen to see voluntary assisted dying legalised throughout Australia. Because a painful and prolonged death – with all the supposed humiliations of being found needy and powerless – reveals too terrible a truth about us: that we're fragile and dependent all our lives *really*, and that whatever honours and plaudits we've won in life, whatever grand story we and others might tell about us, we're likely to die as frail

The Presentation of Christ in the Temple (Candlemas)

creatures with no control and no dignity – except what others are able to bring to our ending through their loving kindness towards us, which we don't reckon to be enough. So, we want to make sure it doesn't come to that. Hence the clamouring for voluntary assisted dying, which I suggest is best understood as an attempt to preserve a narrative of control and independence – about overcoming not death itself but *the power of death*.

That's also why we see "Trump" written in big letters on top of buildings in as many places as possible. And this is why we see the likes of Trump needing to demonstrate their power over others, their greater worth than others, and why they surround themselves with beautiful young women to make them feel that they're not old and unwanted. It's all about the power and fear of death, which can then spread more widely to infect a whole nation.

Even young people experience the power and fear of death; but at a young age it announces itself as FOMO, as the fear of missing out. Or else they fear being unpopular, undesirable, uncool, and unfashionable; hence the epidemic of what René Girard calls *gymnastica nervosa*. And hence today's culture of tattooing among the young, so that their life story can be inscribed on their body in visible form, which is the only permanence that a post-Christian, post-institutional, post-political age can imagine for itself. In all these cases, the power and fear of death is at least partly about the loss of identity, the loss of recognition, the loss of distinctiveness, and the power of this fear makes the world go round.

So, friends, isn't it a wonderful alternative reality that we celebrate here this morning? As Hebrews tells us today, God wades into the midst of our fragile human condition in Jesus Christ, and by facing death in its most shameful and hurtful form, culturally not just physically, the power of death is broken. In that way, as James Alison reminds us, the universally dreaded place of shame is revealed to be habitable after all, and to hold no particular terrors for us. And so say Simeon and Anna, who we meet close to the end of their lives, who know this and who rejoice over it in our gospel today.

And what of us? Every one of us who's known bereavement, or bitter failure, the loss of a marriage, or a job, the collapse of hopes and dreams, the unravelling of a well-established life-narrative, the loss of any sense of purpose, can now inhabit a new narrative, beyond the fear and power of death. The light of Christ shines on us today, as it first shone on us in our baptism, when an identity fit for eternity was given to us as a gift from God in the family of Jesus Christ. The same light shines on us in our Eucharist today – the eternal splendour of God's only son now enlightening our weeks and days – so that what we do here Sunday by Sunday enables us to inhabit the rest of our lives with a quiet fearlessness.

So, with the Psalmist today, we rejoice to find our life established in God's courts and, even if only occasionally, we find with the Psalmist that our heart and our flesh rejoice in the living God. Because even the most fragile little sparrow has its dwelling by right in God's altar, a place of abiding and of generativity, to which Christians make their way week by week in the Eucharist, to be reminded and re-established in that reality. That's why worshippers bow to the altar, and why Catholic priests kiss it at the Eucharist.

Friends, on this feast of Candlemas, the light of Christ shining among us reminds us that the power and fear of death have met their match, that our life and our dignity and our future are safe in God's hands, thanks to Jesus Christ dying and rising among us:

> For the Lord God is a light and a shield,
>   the Lord gives favour and honour:
>   and no good thing will he withhold
>   from those who walk in innocence (Psalm 84:11).

The Lord be with you...

Transfiguration

Transfigured Desire

Transfiguration, 18 February 2007, Year C,
St Paul's, Manuka

Exodus 34:29-35; Psalm 99; 2 Corinthians 3:12-4: 2; Luke 9:28-36

☦ In the Name of the Father and of the Son and of the Holy Spirit. Amen.

Today, on this feast day of the Transfiguration, I want to talk to you about desire and about envy – things we know all too well. And about how the God who transfigures Jesus Christ transfigures our desires, so we become people who can better manage our desires, people less prone to envy and all the trouble it gets us into. Now, if we were Buddhists, it would be a lot easier. We'd have learned from the four noble truths that desire is full of harmful illusions and we'd be following the noble eightfold path to learn the renunciation of desire. We Christians have a more positive view of desire. It helps make us who we are; desire is a goad for us to learn, to achieve, to mate and to thrive. We just have to be careful we're not controlled by desire, and especially by the envy that desire so often descends into. And with the escalation of envy comes violence, and with violence comes the selection of a scapegoat, against whom everyone's desire lines up, and so it goes. No, we have to let the God who transfigures Jesus Christ transfigure our desire so that, as the Church, we can show the world how to live lives of healthy desire beyond envy, rivalry and violence.

The problem with desire is that we don't really desire things, like attractive partners or nice clothes – *not really*. We may not notice something or someone until someone else does, and *then* we see them. Shakespeare was onto this. He's full of stories where the one an admired friend desires becomes the one we desire. And woe betide the one who awakens our desire then becomes an obstacle to it – they become the rival in love, the hated work colleague who helps us dream of advancement then achieves it ahead of us; they become the rival as the colonial master does, who planted the desire for success in the native's mind but prevents the native from ever being as successful as he is. A generation of colonial revolutions in the late twentieth century show how desire gives way to envy then to violence.

In truth, friends, what we desire is not the car or the girl, not the promotion or the public accolade. What we desire is the model of our desire, the person who awakens these desires in us. We want what they've got: we want their poise, their cool self-sufficiency, their mojo, their sex appeal, or whatever it is we feel we lack. All desire is desire for the being of someone else, the person who becomes the model of our desire. This is how we make idols of others – of sporting heroes, of film stars, or of airhead celebrities who do nothing except act as the focus of others' desires. And if you don't believe me, ask yourself why it is that achieving our desires often fails to satisfy us.

Gaining the object of our desire seldom really satisfies because our desire is really about the person who mediates to us our desire for that object. If Paris Hilton stops wearing lo-rider jeans, for instance, countless girls won't feel like wearing them anymore. If we buy ourselves a leather jacket just like the one Tom Cruise wore in *Top Gun*, then we'll feel at least a bit disappointed, because we're still not Tom Cruise. Friends, this is how advertising works. It presents attractive and interesting people and lifestyles to awaken our desire for something, which we promptly go out and buy. And because the thing itself doesn't really satisfy, we're primed by our desire to respond to the next advert, going out to buy something else, *ad infinitum*.

Another group of people who mediate desires to us are religious leaders. Perhaps it's their spiritual powers we admire, their faith, or their wisdom. Many people make idols of their religious leaders

– their television evangelist of choice, or Pope John Paul, or the Bhagwan. But when we draw close to these religious leaders, rivalry can set in; we can feel that what they have prevents us from having it. Awestruck regard can quickly become rivalrous and resentful, if the religious leader doesn't help us find the peace or the poise or the wisdom that we envy in them, or if they actively harm us in the spiritual life. Hence the regular glee in religious circles when some spiritual celebrity falls flat in public, caught out in a scandal; hence also the rise of official complaints and recriminations in congregation after congregation within Australian Anglicanism, as a needy generation craves more and more from its religious leaders and comes to feel disappointed, because they're not getting what they're convinced the leader should be delivering.

Now this is a long introduction, but I think it's necessary to help understand the emphasis in today's readings on Moses veiling his face, and about Jesus transfigured for all his companions to see, not just one. Let me tell you what I mean.

Moses is the great witness of the old covenant, and as he looks upon God, the model of his desire, he comes to reflect the being of God, to share in the glory of God, and so his face shines. But only Moses, not the rest of the people. Their encounter with God is mediated. They see the glory of God in the face of Moses, not for themselves. Their desire for God is mediated by Moses, and hence the risk of envy and resentment enters in. I can't think of another explanation for why Moses covers his face when he meets with the people, so they don't see it shining. He doesn't want to rub their noses in it, and risk arousing their envy and rivalry if he disappoints them as every religious leader inevitably must. Whenever the desire of others guides our desire, whenever we live derivatively through idols, or through the opponents that those we respect can turn into, then we're never truly free. But God has something more in store for us, and this is what the New Testament testifies.

In our 2 Corinthians reading today, Paul is weary of all this mediated religion. This is the glory that's being set aside, the last gasp of business as usual, as Paul tells us. The veil that remains for so many people, according to Paul today, refers to the mediated nature of their desire, to the derivative nature of their lives, their yearnings, of their faith even. But for Paul we no longer have to look to others to find ourselves. We no longer have to take our empty buckets of need to the well of another's being to have them filled. We don't have to live in the shadow of others – as victims, for instance, or as people dominated by their envy of others so that our whole lives are given over to conflict, like all those anti-American terrorists on the world stage, or like your typical obsessed gossip in whichever workplace or community group.

We don't have to live in the desires of marketers who endlessly manipulate us, and the whole cast of our adult lives need no longer be set by the sibling rivalry of our childhood. The freedom of the Spirit to which Paul invites us in 2 Corinthians today is the transfiguration of our desire, and it comes from a God who reveals God's self to all of us, to you and to me, not just to a great mediator like Moses. In Jesus Christ, we all have direct access to God, and this is the message of our Gospel this morning.

There's Moses and there's Elijah, the great messengers of old, but they see no more than Peter, James and John see, and no more than we see. They see God's glory in the face of Jesus Christ, and so do we. Poor Peter doesn't get it, though. He thinks Jesus is on par with Moses and Elijah – hence his offer to build three little pagodas for three equal gurus. But God leaves no doubt. The God who spoke from a cloud in the Old Testament speaks again, and this literary device is quite clear. Jesus is God with us, with all of us, and so the age of mediated religion is over. Peter doesn't get it until the resurrection, when the old mediated desire that clings anxiously to being because of the fear of death has finally collapsed with Jesus on the cross, only to be reborn invincibly for Peter beyond death in the resurrection.

Certainly, something greater than Moses is here. Jesus' desire is for God and for us. If we imitate him, we're imitating one who isn't big-noting himself, who isn't any threat to us. So, if Jesus is our mediator, we come to share his desire for God and for souls. The only rivalry this leads to is the wish to outdo each other in showing love and respect. The only violence this leads to is the violence of our aversion to living half a life, dictated to by the desires of others who we alternately idolise and demonise.

This is why we have the Church – to be a community of transfigured desire, sharing equally the glory of God revealed to all of us in the face of Jesus Christ. This is why we have the Eucharist, so the glory of God streaming out of the elevated host illuminates all our faces equally, and so all share the one desire with Jesus, which honours God and honours human beings, beyond living derivatively, enviously and violently. This is why Eucharistic worship together matters, and not just some prayer service – or "café church", or some other gimmick that reduces the Gospel to another consumer option.

Because only in the Eucharist do we ascend the holy mountain together, Sunday by Sunday, to witness the transfiguration of Jesus who then realigns our hearts like a powerful, healing magnet. And thus, we experience the transfiguration of our own desires. Hence Eucharistic Christianity becomes for us a mystical path to a renewed moral life, as we find we're no longer people dominated by neediness, by envy, by rivalry and the violent desires that so typically fuel the old way of being religious – the way that's passing away, as Paul explains to us today.

Paul tells us today that where the Spirit of the Lord is, there is freedom. There is a transfigured desire that reveals who we most truly are as we see the glory of God reflected in ourselves – in a mirror, as Paul puts it. Thus, God frees us to live passionately, confidently, as non-rivalrous and non-violent people. Paul himself testifies to this effect today. He doesn't play the politics of favourites or sweet talk people or act with cunning against opponents but is very direct in his ministry, leaving the rest to God. In all of this, we see the glory of God in the face of Jesus Christ at work, mediating a transfigured desire that we share in every Eucharist.

The Lord be with you...

All in Good Time

Transfiguration, 26 February 2017, Year A,
All Saints', Ainslie,
Exodus 24:12-18; Psalm 2; 2 Peter 1:16-21; Matthew 17:1-9

† In the Name of the Father and of the Son and of the Holy Spirit. Amen.

One of the things I remember about growing up is being impatient. I was impatient to get my hands on the steering wheel of a car, for instance, and the long wait until my 17th birthday seemed interminable. I was impatient to have my first girlfriend, too, but I won't go into the details of that. Later, I was impatient as a slow learner of the recorder, with fingering exercises and painfully slow passages of Handel sonatas eventually becoming more fluid, and occasionally all of a sudden, but not without long preparation. This was also true a few years back when I had to learn to read French, so I could work my way through untranslated René Girard with a dictionary. I've forgotten a lot of it now, but back then I can remember the little breakthroughs, including having my first dream in French! As a scholar and writer, I'm in the breakthrough business, but it all takes such a long time.

    Recently, I've been revisiting my research notebooks from ten years back and there I find ideas set out that have only much more recently become firmly settled in my mind – in other words, I knew about things that I didn't fully appreciate. You all know what I'm saying. Life and years and experience and exposure eventually bring us to see new things, to develop new capacities, and there's no other way for it. In our age of microwave cookery, it's good to be reminded that real flavour comes from a slow cooker.

Friends, it's like this with our God, too, who is more patient than we often are, and who transforms us bit by bit over a lifetime: in wisdom, in faith, in discipleship, in our moral capacities, in our ability to love. God knows the sort of creatures we are, and better than we do. As individuals, as cultures, as a Church, we humans build on the past, yet we rub up against all sorts of new experiences and challenges at every stage, and this back-and-forth is how we eventually become who we are. Of course, there are breakthroughs, sudden insights, overnight conversions, but these are part of a continuing process, and we shouldn't despise the overall slowness. God is in the slow cooking business, and the flavour doesn't develop any other way.

Now, all this is by way of introducing today's theme of the Transfiguration, which these days we celebrate in its proper location at the end of this post-Christmas season of Epiphany. Today marks the great moment when Jesus' true identity is revealed to his disciples – even though trusty Peter doesn't quite get it, and in Peter's confusion the rest of us Christians can take comfort.

God's preparation for this moment was a long one. In our Exodus reading today, we see Moses ascending a mountain, up where the pagans always liked to go in times before him, and there he meets Israel's God. We know it's Israel's God not least by two important numbers that are woven into the story – the six days that Moses was in the cloud, recalling the six days of creation from Genesis, and the forty days he stayed up there, recalling Israel's forty years of wandering in the wilderness. Here we see God's investment over time being recalled and recapitulated, until, at last, the law can be revealed and understood. We hear another Old Testament witness in our Psalm this morning, with God's power over the nations revealed from heaven. The divine claim that Moses recognises, built on all that's been revealed to Israel, is now declared to be universal, and I'll come back to that idea.

Now, you won't have missed the connections between our Exodus reading today and Matthew's Gospel account of Jesus'

Transfiguration. We're again up a mountain, and again there's a cloud of God's presence. Moses is there, but also Elijah, representing later Old Testament history (and who's also associated with the mountain of God). But whereas Moses' face was shining when he eventually came down the mountain with the ten commandments, in today's Gospel Jesus is positively incandescent, solar, nuclear, to emphasise that something far greater is here – though it's something that only makes sense in light of God's long preparations with Moses, Elijah and the entire Old Testament. This is why the Gospels, and especially Matthew, present Jesus as the fulfilment of the law and the prophets: because this is how God reveals the truth to creatures with developing minds like ours, and who live within history, as we do.

But, of course, poor old Peter doesn't quite get it. He thinks history is over, and that it's time to build Crown Casino on the mountain top, so everyone can settle back to enjoy the good times. He's like Jamie Packer at Barangaroo – or like Francis Fukuyama, who thinks that global capitalism represents the final flowering of history. Peter also seems to be thinking that Jesus is simply on par with Moses and Elijah, hence the three wings of the casino that he wants to build, one for each of them.

No, it's not time to settle down. Jesus clearly has more work to do, so he takes his disciples back down the mountain: back to the real world, to history, and to the mission. This is where the truth of Jesus' Transfiguration will finally dawn, in the rough and tumble. Indeed, Jesus tells them not to let on about his Transfiguration until after the resurrection – because without that last piece of the story in place they won't have the full picture, and God's revelation won't be properly understood. Jesus knows our limitations, and he works with them.

There's one more thing I've noticed this time around, reflecting on the Transfiguration in Matthew, and it has to do with this central Christian proclamation of Jesus as Son of God – the recognition of God's radical personal investment in creation and in humanity through Jesus. I notice that this message appears three times in Matthew. The first time, God declares it from heaven when Jesus is baptised by John the Baptist (Matthew 3:17). Today, once again, we hear the heavenly voice in the story of Jesus' Transfiguration, declaring who Jesus is to the disciples.

God is making the point over and over, and in different contexts, until we eventually get it. And of course, this strategy is fulfilled in spades with the third declaration of Jesus' divine sonship in Matthew's Gospel. And where does it appear? (The clergy present are no doubt right onto it!) It appears again at the end of Jesus' crucifixion, when Matthew has an earthquake and the tombs are opened, and the resurrection birth pangs are already underway on Good Friday. At this point, the Roman Centurion and his companions declare the truth, that "truly this man was the Son of God" (Matthew 27:54). In other words, the Gospel begins with God's revelation of who God is and who Jesus is, and by the end even the pagans are declaring it. Friends, this is God's patient work, God's slow-cooking revelation, finally served up and ready for the whole world to appreciate.

Now, what about you and me? Where does our own slow, even faltering progress fit into this story? Where is our journey of faith – a journey that's sometimes more, sometimes less associated with the Church and its worship; a sense of progress that's sometimes clear, sometimes uncertain, always hard won, and apparently never quite finished? We're helped here by today's Epistle, with its very Catholic presentation of how you and I are nurtured in the faith until we eventually truly make that faith our own. The writer, who we say is Peter because he refers to the Transfiguration as an eyewitness in today's Epistle, explains how he expects that our faith will be nurtured and grown. He refers to his testimony among the apostles, who were participants in the events of Jesus' life, passing down their witness to us.

They didn't make it up, he tells us; it's not a clever myth, and it's not anybody's own interpretation. Rather, it's God's work through the events themselves, as mediated by the apostles' authoritative testimony. So it is, friends, in the apostolic Church to which we belong as Anglicans, with its bishops and saints and theologians, and with all those faithful Christian witnesses down the millennia who confirm the truth of who Jesus is and how he transforms lives.

Now, the point of this Catholic talk isn't to offend Protestants, and to make Church authority primary over personal experience. Rather, today's Epistle sets the scene and clears the way for personal experience. The key passage that helps us understand this is when Peter refers to our own eventual embrace of the authoritative message that he and the apostles proclaim: "You will do well to be attentive to this as to a lamp shining in a dark place, until the day dawns and the morning star rises in *your* hearts" (2 Peter 1:19b).

As we participate in the Church, as we sit under the word of God week by week, as we share in the Eucharistic celebration, and as we learn the habits and the stories and the disciplines of Christian life, so eventually the light dawns in our own hearts and makes this faith our own. This is how we come to acknowledge and to own what has always been ours but which we might never have fully inhabited – that way, with this morning star now visible, at the dawn of a new stage in our life, we can become fellow witnesses with the saints to the apostolic faith. It's not immediate, it's certainly not without long preparation – it's not without the shaping, guiding hand of the Church; and it's not without further steps remaining on the journey.

Friends, as the Epiphany of Jesus Christ flares up with transfiguring brilliance in our Gospel today, so might we see that light shining in the midst of this Eucharist that we celebrate, and in the faces of God's beloved people gathered here. And if this vision isn't bright and compelling for us, let's resolve to persevere, to pray for the breakthroughs to come, and to wait in patience. The smell of God's slow cooking is delicious, and we're meant to get a whiff of it here in the Eucharist.

The Lord be with you ...

Passion Sunday (Palm Sunday)

Topsy Turvy

Palm Sunday (Passion Sunday), 1 April 2007, Year C,
St Paul's Manuka

Liturgy of the Palms: Luke 19:28-40; Psalm 118:1-2, 19-29
Liturgy of the Eucharist: Isaiah 50:4-9a; Psalm 31:9-18;
Philippians 2:5-11; Luke 23:1-49

† In the Name of the Father and of the Son and of the Holy Spirit. Amen.

In 1999, Jim Broadbent and Allan Corduner starred as Gilbert and Sullivan in a film about the life and work of this extraordinary partnership. The film was called *Topsy Turvy*, which was a name the pair used for the imaginative world they created in their productions. After all, the world of G and S is hardly the world of sober, practical realism, is it, with ordinary characters and predictable outcomes? Perhaps this is why people loved it so much, as an alternative to the grind of life in a newly industrialised era belonging increasingly to the clock and to the production line.

Today on this Palm Sunday, this Passion Sunday, we're introduced to another topsy turvy world. Those well-meaning souls who tell us that Christianity is an entirely reasonable set of values miss the topsy turvy in today's Scripture readings. Because today we don't see our familiar values reflected back to us; we don't receive the kind of reassurance for our established habits of mind that many seek from the Church. Instead, we enter the topsy turvy world of Jesus and his passion.

At the heart of today's readings is the sense that as Jesus goes to the cross, the order of things in our world is turned upside down. This is why the passion gospel from Luke imagines the sky darkened, accompanying the apocalyptic warning from Jesus that business as usual in society was being put on notice by the events of his passion: "Daughters of Jerusalem, do not weep for me, but weep for yourselves and for your children. For the days are surely coming when they will say, 'Blessed are the barren, and the wombs that never bore, and the breasts that never nursed'. Then they will begin to say to the mountains, 'Fall on us'; and to the hills, 'Cover us'". In other words, "no longer will you be able to solve your problems by scapegoating the likes of me", says Jesus, "and then go home all smug and satisfied". Because the death and resurrection of Jesus upsets and undermines the way all human societies solve their problems, manage change and cope with the anxieties of life. Only the peace of Christ will work now, not the cynical pragmatism that's served us so well in the past.

This encroaching world of topsy turvy is also evident in the way human worth is recast in our readings today. The thief on the cross is the lowest of the low, suffering a shameful end to a shameful life. But in opening his heart to Jesus, without seeking to justify himself, he receives the greatest promise of the New Testament: "today you will be with me in paradise". Jesus himself leads the way in this revaluing of human worth. Where a conquering Roman General would have entered Jerusalem on a fine horse, Jesus enters on a donkey, almost as a parody. The crowd cheers him as a political messiah, a military liberator perhaps, but Jesus knows what's coming and opts instead for powerlessness.

This is the nature of Jesus' true greatness, as Paul knows, in today's critical passage from Philippians, about God's self-emptying in Jesus, and about Jesus emptying himself so that God's greatness could be seen through his human humility. Jesus is also taking-up the role of suffering servant from Isaiah today, the role of faithful Israel in every generation, showing that greatness in God's eyes involves bearing the burdens of others, and bearing the burden of truth – also bearing the weight of grief, as Psalm 31 unforgettably names it today, not looking for life to be easier or more straightforward than it really is.

So, friends, in the topsy turvy world that we enter today with Jesus and his passion, we find ourselves lifted out of the reasonable, the conventional and the familiar. Jesus knows that the tectonic plates of reality are shifting. He knows that a deep vein in the order of things has been tapped, and that a great, joyous energy is being released. Didn't we hear it loud and clear in today's Gospel of the Palms: "Some of the Pharisees in the crowd said to him, 'Teacher, order your disciples to stop'. He answered, 'I tell you, if these were silent, the stones would shout out.'"

Friends, the stones are crying out in our Eucharist today: the living stones that you and I are. By virtue of our baptism, as St Paul reminds us, we're set up on Jesus the great cornerstone – the great bearer of burdens, that is, and giver of orientation. And if, heaven forbid, we fail to find the joy, and the proud, public confidence to advance this Christian faith in our generation, at least the stones of our fine Church building will cry out in witness to Christ here in Manuka, awaiting a Rector and a congregation who can join them in their song. But, of course, of course, a good outcome is ultimately inevitable, because the topsy turvy breakthrough of Easter is absolutely unstoppable – with our help, yours and mine, or without it.

The Lord be with you...

Returning to Our True Country

Passion Sunday (Palm Sunday), 24 March 2013, Year C,
All Saints, Ainslie

Liturgy of the Palms: Luke 19:28-40; Psalm 118:1-2, 19-29
Liturgy of the Eucharist: Isaiah 50:4-9a; Psalm 31:9-18;
Philippians 2:5-11; Luke 23:1-49

† In the Name of the Father and of the Son and of the Holy Spirit. Amen.

Friends, from today and through Holy Week, then across the Easter Weekend, we Christians return to our true country. The world in which we currently make our home is not our true country, in the sense that as Christians we can never be entirely at home here – because it's a world of violence and the abuse of power, and it runs on the fuel of shame and fear, and it secures its preferred version of peace by the sacrificial mechanism of scapegoating. We saw this world doing what comes naturally to it here in Canberra through the week, with a new peace secured at the cost of significant bloodletting in the government. The same mechanism has led the other side of politics to revisit some old imagery of sacrifice with its call to "ditch the witch", unable to cope with a feisty female Prime Minister in Julia Gillard. And if it's not the witch, then it's asylum seekers and foreign workers that they can't abide.

Friends, our baptism makes us citizens of another country, of a different world. With relief we learn the language and habits of our true country through the time-honoured practices of liturgical worship, of prayer, and through growing familiarity with the story of God's people from Scripture. In our readings for this Palm Sunday, this Passion Sunday, we travel deep into the culture of our

Passion Sunday (Palm Sunday)

true country, of our Christian belonging, and from this perspective the truth about things in the world around us, the world of our exile, becomes a lot clearer. Let me show you what I mean.

First, I'm going to talk to you about the way our world runs on sacrifice, which today's Gospel readings bring to light. In our Gospel of the Palms, Jesus is so popular on his entry into Jerusalem, isn't he? He's the King who is to come. And in the main Gospel reading for today, Pilate, the Roman governor, is most anxious about this: a King to threaten the kingship of Caesar! Then Jesus is sent to Herod, the puppet King of Rome's Judean province – the one who would no doubt prefer to be King in his own right but who must be content with the scrap of authority that Rome has thrown him. But Jesus doesn't play this game of thrones. He deconstructs the power of kingship by riding into Jerusalem on a donkey, and he refuses to accept the title of King as Pilate presses it on him: "so you are a King then". Later, in the company of that also-ran, Herod, Pilate's enemy, Jesus says not a word, so unwilling is he to join in this rivalry between Herod and Pilate.

And here we can see the mechanism of sacrifice revealed. The crowd that goes berserk as it welcomes Jesus into Jerusalem is the same crowd that quickly turns on Jesus, baying for his blood. Hence, I wonder if Jesus' comment as he rides by the affronted scribes and Pharisees – about the stones crying out – is meant to be ironic. I wonder if Jesus might be referring to stones as the implements of sacrifice, of death by stoning. Might Jesus be saying that the crowd will soon stop praising him, and turn instead to sacrifice, to the equivalent of stoning? After all, this has happened to Jesus before in Luke's Gospel, in Chapter 4, when another enthusiastic crowd welcomed Jesus at the Nazareth synagogue but then swiftly turned on him and tried to push him off a cliff – that other favourite ancient method of sacrifice, the Nazareth version of Rome's Tarpeian Rock.

Two other very clear images of scapegoating can be found in today's Gospel of the Passion, also from Luke. There's the little reference to Pilate and Herod becoming friends, where before they'd been enemies. They'd essentially been rival claimants to Kingship, and hence they were anxious about Jesus as a third claimant. Their newfound friendship shows how scapegoating Jesus brings peace and settles things down. The other image comes in the release of Barabbas, who really was a rival claimant for power, a knife man, a terrorist who had actually threatened Rome's power. Yet here the guilty one is let off while Jesus is condemned. Jesus' innocence, which even the hard-bitten Roman Centurion recognises at the foot of the cross, doesn't stop him from being scapegoated. Because scapegoating the innocent is the usual price of peace and good order in the so-called real world – the world, that is, where you and I normally live.

And, friends, all this is so ingrained that we're not even aware of it. That's why Jesus prays his remarkable prayer from the cross: "Father forgive them, for they don't know what they're doing". It's not that they're monsters, or especially evil. They've just learned to read from a particular script, to live in the grip of a particular system. Jesus' forgiveness, however – his offer of peace as the first words out of his mouth at the resurrection – means that a new world is dawning, in which violence and exclusion aren't the only response to shame and threat. Instead, Jesus' God is no threat, no competitor, within the dynamics of our world as it is. Rather, through the cross of Jesus, in the teeth of shame and failure as this world assesses it, God begins to completely undo this world, and to reveal our true country, where we join the risen Christ through our baptism, and where we start to experience a peace from God not as the world gives – in other words, the peace of God which passes all understanding.

Friends, we see the end of this old world evoked in today's Gospel of the Passion. Jesus' speech to the women of Jerusalem is the first sign of this, warning them of the way things are going to start unravelling in their world now that he's come to his cross – now that the unstable, fragile nature of their old world is being revealed. The darkening of the sun at noon, and the tearing of the temple curtain, are further apocalyptic signs; the old world is cast into darkness and the sacrificial factory of the temple is torn through, so God can no longer be kept at a safe distance by the world that's busy crucifying God's son.

Before the cross of Jesus, God was regularly misunderstood and misrepresented. We see this mistaken view among those present at Jesus' crucifixion. The God they all believed in ought to come in power to rescue Jesus: the bystanders call out for this in mockery, and even the thief on the cross joins in. He's eager to prove that he too is still one of the crowd, and hence to moderate his own shameful exclusion by adding to Jesus' shame and exclusion.

But this popular, all-powerful god, who favours redemptive violence and who underwrites our liking for vendetta and payback, is silent. That god is dead, thank God, and revealed to be dead by Jesus on the cross. Our God, the true God, certainly does triumph on the cross, but it's a different kind of triumph. Our God doesn't triumph by turning the tables in this world's time-honoured fashion. Rather, our God triumphs by revealing a new beginning beyond the power of shame and violence that keeps people docile and compliant. This is the God who reassured his suffering servant in Isaiah today, and the Psalmist, too, whose cry from the depths is not an abject cry, because he's learned to trust the power of God's counter-story against the world's more popular story of power and success. The cross of Jesus is the truly triumphant revealing of this reality, of this new country with its different rules, and with its new language for success and for power.

The so-called Christ hymn from Philippians today puts it so beautifully. Christ humbles himself by joining us in solidarity under the heel of brute reality, thanks to the peerless technology of shame, fear, and violent social control that crucifixion represented. By entering that darkest of places and undergoing that most comprehensive of deaths, Jesus revealed God's absolute loving solidarity with us in the midst of even the worst horrors that we humans have concocted. And from that place everything changes. From that place Jesus is raised up by God the Father and made Lord over all things, given the name that is above every other name. And, of course, this is no exclusive, assertive and rivalrous claim on Jesus' part from our familiar world of us versus them. Rather, it's an inclusive uniqueness; it's a special calling in which you and I join Jesus as proud insiders of a country that demands no outsiders, in a belonging that demands no exclusion, and in a suffering love that leads to no bitterness or payback.

Hence, we begin a week of pilgrimage back to our true country. We hear a strange and wonderful language that we risk forgetting, we recall the old stories, and we reacquaint ourselves with the sacramental food that's so different from what we have to gnaw on and choke on in what we call our "normal" lives. And so, friends, we remember who and whose we are, and the dream that Christians hold fast, which changes everything if we let it. Then, when we return from this Holy Week and Easter journey, for another year back in that world where shame and fear, where envy and violence reign, and where scapegoating is the best answer anyone manages to come up with, we can find the wherewithal to live and to dream and to hope and to act differently.

The Lord be with you...

The Darkness of God?

Palm Sunday (Passion Sunday), 9 April 2017, Year A,
St James', King Street, Sydney

Isaiah 50:4-9a, Psalm 31:9-18; Philippians 2:5-11, Matthew 27:11-54

✝ In the Name of the Father and of the Son and of the Holy Spirit. Amen.

Now from the sixth hour there was darkness over all the land unto the ninth hour. And about the ninth hour Jesus cried with a loud voice, saying 'Eli, Eli, lama sabacthani?' That is to say, 'My God, my God, why hast though forsaken me?' (Matthew 27:45-46).

Today, our theme is darkness and godforsakenness. And what more relevant theme could there be for so many people in today's Western world? The loss of a secure identity, of certainties from yesterday and hope for tomorrow, is spawning anxiety and anger everywhere. Brexit, the election of Trump, and the far right's rise in Australia reveal in public what's also true in private. In the angst of many girls and young women over body image, to the desperation of ice addiction, to the resignation of a generation of Australians that will never achieve home ownership, we see the loss of hope. Likewise, the inescapable sufferings of brute reality cast a pall of darkness and wretchedness over many lives. Every priest knows that personal loss and life's disappointments often leave people groping in the dark and feeling godforsaken. We've learned to equate God's presence with security, confidence, success, happiness, insidership, to the extent that losing these fragile and fleeting comforts can seem like the death of God.

But I want to suggest a different take on all this, in light of today's readings. Here we find a God at work despite this darkness, and intimately present despite the sense of God's absence. This is a message that the Christian mystical tradition has long emphasised, with its cloud of unknowing, with its deep and dazzling darkness. But it should be common property for all Christians, as we find it to be throughout Scripture, and not least in our readings today.

I want to put a particular spin on this paradox of God's absence and presence today, in light of two great modern thinkers: Friedrich Nietzsche and René Girard. My insight is that the darkness of God, the eclipse of God, the godforsakenness that's become a defining feature of modern secular experience, is in fact the death of an inadequate, older, human-centred view of God – a confected, sociological sacred, and not the real God at all. The god we miss today, who seems to have deserted us, is the god who helped unify a civilization, to identify and curse its necessary class of deviants, and to mark its outsiders, so that we knew who the insiders were. This god, now disappearing in darkness, once allowed us to have a common enemy, so that we could all feel unified. This was a god who underwrote our success, our insidership, our identity, our worth, allowing us to feel special – of course, in contrast with others who weren't.

In his book *The Gay Science*, Nietzsche offers his famous aphorism #125 about the death of what I think is this old god. It's a passage that's often misunderstood. Nietzsche's fictional madman comes into the town square, prophetically declaring that we've killed this old god, and that as a result we're bearing the consequences. We've lost the old certainties. Nietzsche's madman asks, "What were we doing when we unchained this earth from its sun? Whither is it moving now? Whither are we moving? Away from all suns? Are we not plunging continually? Backward, sideward, forward, in all directions? Is there still any up or down? Are we not straying as through an infinite nothing? Do we not feel the breath of empty space? Has it not become colder? Is not night continually closing in on us?"[2]

René Girard argues that the god whose death Nietzsche declares is the old, sociological sacred that every human culture confects in its own way, but always to secure a stable unity at the expense of some targeted violence. The disappearance of *this* god is what Nietzsche is lamenting, believing that – through Christianity – the modern West has lost something indispensable, something strong and violent, something Dionysian, which we need to get back: "What festivals of atonement, what sacred games shall we have to invent?"[3]

But, of course, the god Nietzsche wants back is far closer to the sacred pretensions of Hitler and the Third Reich than it is to the humility of Jesus who went to the cross, who emptied himself, taking the form of a slave, as we read in our Epistle today. Nietzsche would have scorned the honest lament of today's Psalm, too. And he'd make nothing of today's Isaiah reading – he'd think that the godly one, the contemplative, active teacher that Isaiah gives us there, the suffering servant, could only be deluded: as if knowing God could actually entail the weakness and shame of exile from the sacred circle; as if this darkness of God could be a blessing from God.

No, we worship a different God. Ours is the God that Nietzsche rejected because he preferred the pagan Dionysus over the crucified Christ. Nietzsche knew that thanks to the Bible, and thanks especially to Jesus, the old gods have been culturally routed and undermined, and he's not happy about it. As far as he's concerned, we Christians have murdered the only god worth having. Hence the darkness and the godforsakenness of our modern Western experience – according to Nietzsche – because the strength and the violent certainty has all drained away.

---

2 Friedrich Nietzsche, *The Gay Science*, trans Walter Kaufmann (1882) (New York: Vintage, 1974), 181-82.
3 Ibid, 181.

Friends, as we hear Matthew's passion story today, we step into this darkness and god-forsakenness, and we're introduced to a different God, to the real God: the God of Isaiah, and the Psalmist; the God of Jesus Christ. This is the God that Nietzsche despised, who he regards as having ruined everything, whose baleful influence needs to be expunged – and didn't we modern Westerners give that our best shot in the uniquely blood-soaked twentieth century? I'm now going to take a walk with you through Matthew's passion narrative that was sung for us by the choir, to show you what I mean.

Today's passion narrative is about human communities doing what comes naturally. Envy and rivalry are to the fore; we read that Pilate was well aware that envy on the part of religious authorities had delivered Jesus to him. Indeed, the whole thing starts with Judas' failed bid to force Jesus' hand, to make him take on the system, the controlling nexus of culture and religion, only to realise that he'd got everything completely wrong. Judas, like Nietzsche, preferred the old, more violent god. But where Nietzsche went mad when he could no longer avoid Christ's claim, Judas hanged himself. And then, friends, with envy and escalating tensions, the obvious, age-old solution presents itself: let's lynch someone to unify the factions and to restore peace. So, we see the chief priests and elders actually whipping up the mob, calling for Barabbas to be released – even though he was a bandit, a terrorist – so that Jesus could be sacrificed.

Now isn't this interesting? Why release someone who's a real danger, and crucify someone who's non-violent? Likewise, why obsess about the relatively minor threat of terrorism while ignoring today's major threats of epidemic obesity, rampant youth suicide, nuclear weapons, and climate change? Why live with an acceptable level of corruption while whistle blowers represent such a threat? Why tolerate child abusers among the clergy while driving out priests who upset key egos among the laity, or make things uncomfortable for the bishop?

This is all because we need the usual suspects to keep the system going. We can cope with terrorists, paedophiles and corrupt officials because they're so like the rest of us that by damning them we don't have to face the truth about ourselves. Whereas prophets show up the whole system and leave us nowhere to hide. We can cope with difference, even welcome it, as long as it doesn't reveal that we're all really basically the same! And this is what we see in today's Passion narrative: we see business as usual, with sacred wrath turned on Jesus while leaving the system in place. All its necessary structural rivalries, which are symbolised by Barabbas, are preserved, and him too – but not Jesus, who's the bigger threat.

The difference in this story, compared with all the myths of pagan religion, is that Jesus' innocence is declared openly rather than concealed: declared by Judas, by Pilate's wife, by Pilate himself, and even by the execution party, which takes some pity on Jesus – they try to be at least a bit decent to him, getting him some help carrying his cross, and sharing their rough soldiers' brew with him when he's thirsty. This is because the Bible begins to reveal the truth about scapegoating. Instead of being the incarnation of evil and entirely deserving a sacrificial death, sacrificial victims emerge in the Bible as innocent.

This is what we heard in our Psalm today, and in that passage from Isaiah. So, while everyone's against Jesus – the religious leaders, the mob, the soldiers who mock him, even the thieves crucified with him who seize their last chance to be part of a group consensus – yet the chorus of condemnation isn't uniform. Something's changed. The sacrifice is underway, as ever, but it can no longer work as would have been expected. The consensus is starting to unravel. An alternative is presenting itself in this passion text, a God beyond groupthink and cathartic sacrifice.

Notice the way the tables are being turned throughout this passion narrative. The soldiers mock Jesus as king, but it's really the authoritative structure of kingship and the control it represents that's being mocked by Jesus. Likewise, the accusation set over his head on the cross, "This is the King of the Jews", is at the same time both a Roman charge of wrongdoing and a divinely revealed truth. Thus we see that the old order is indeed slipping into darkness. And Jesus himself shows that he rejects the whole system in the way he replies to Pilate or doesn't reply. Pilate asks him is he is a king, to locate Jesus one way or another in the familiar world of rivalries that's at stake here. But Jesus refuses to buy into it: "Thou sayest", is all he offers, which is much like saying "whatever". Jesus is telling Pilate that, however he chooses to construe this situation, Jesus couldn't care less – it's nothing to do with him and with what's important to him.

Then, friends, the darkness comes on symbolically in the narrative. Here, Matthew uses meteorology to point to theology. I suggest that here it's the old sacred, the age-old system, humanity's business as usual, that goes into eclipse. Jesus is now at the deepest point of his immersion in our human world, and in his cry of God-forsakenness he prefigures Nietzsche's madman by 1900 years. A world well under control, and the angry god such a world relies on, are going into eclipse. Jesus dies to usher in a new beginning for the world with God.

And this new world is not slow in revealing itself. The temple curtain is torn in two – the temple that the chief priests were so eager to protect, with all it stood for, by refusing to accept Judas' tainted pieces of silver back into the temple treasury. What's more, Matthew gives us the extraordinary scene of graves opened and the victims of history returning large as life – a breakout that theologian Jürgen Moltmann called "the resurrection of the disappeared, the murdered and the gassed". And the final word goes to the pagans, who come to see the truth about Jesus: that the one they condemned, mocked and killed, the one who sank into death under the darkness and absence of God, really was God with us. God's declaration at Jesus' baptism and his Transfiguration is now echoed on the lips of a pagan Centurion and his death squad:

Passion Sunday (Palm Sunday)

"Truly this was the Son of God". Friends, the times, they are a changin'!

So, despite darkness and God's absence, despite the loss of control and stability that our civilization nostalgically hankers after, despite the failed promises of success and lost hopes of restored fortunes that have left so many people feeling adrift and angry, despite much personal loss and cultural confusion, all of which Friedrich Nietzsche lamented, here we encounter a different story, a different reality, a different God. And this week, Monday to Friday, then next Sunday, you and I will be meeting this God in the only place possible: in word and sacrament, in darkness and what seems to the uninitiated to be God's absence.

The Lord be with you ...

Holy Thursday (Maundy Thursday)

Jesus' Alternative Sacrifice

Holy Thursday (Maundy Thursday), 13 April 2017,
St James', King Street, Sydney

Exodus 12:1-4, 11-14; Psalm 116:1-2, 11-18;
1 Corinthians 11:23-26; John 13:1-17, 31b-35

† In the Name of the Father and of the Son and of the Holy Spirit. Amen.

I want to talk to you tonight about sacrifice – what it is and what it isn't – in light of our readings and of the Eucharist we celebrate. Paul and John give us two versions of Jesus' sacrifice tonight.

In our Epistle, from Paul, Jesus gives *himself*; he doesn't point the finger at someone else as the world's problem, who needs to be sacrificed, but he gives himself with his own hand. This is about God taking responsibility. And, what's more, Jesus tells us that this is about remembering, whereas sacrifices are more typically meant to be forgotten once their work is done, aren't they? The bodies are meant to stay buried. Likewise, yesterday's heroes, now discredited, are airbrushed from the photos in the next edition of the history textbooks, as was the case with Trotsky and others in Stalin's Russia. For René Girard, myths are about remembering the pacifying effect of scapegoating sacrifice, while keeping the truth of such sacrifice under wraps. For Jesus, however, if the system requires a sacrifice, he'll be that sacrifice himself. But where the system requires forgetting, he'll insist that we remember.

In John's Gospel tonight, we have another take on Jesus' sacrifice. John's version of the Easter events makes it clear that Jesus is sacrificed at the same time as the Passover lambs, so the link with the sacrificial past is made. But, unlike the other Gospels, John doesn't give us the bread and wine of the last supper. Instead he gives us Jesus' sacrifice in a different key, with a remarkable piece of political theatre.

In Jesus' act of foot washing, he upends traditional hierarchies – slaves washed feet, or women did, while here it's the master and lord who takes the towel. Yet this action means glorification rather than humiliation for Jesus, because it reveals what God is like – a God who's for us, a God who'll do what it takes to get through to our hardened hearts. Likewise – and this may come as a surprise – we infer that Jesus also washes the feet of Judas, who is to betray him. There's no payback here, no hatred for Judas, yet Jesus' act is the most profound critique of what Judas is doing. Judas exhibits the imagination of this world, trying to force Jesus' hand and resolve the problems of Israel through conflict with the Romans. But Jesus enacts God's response to human narrow-mindedness, vindictiveness and hurt pride, which is to absorb it like a sponge until there's nothing of it left. Once again, if it's self-justifying violence we want, Jesus instead submits to self-justifying violence, while showing us the alternative.

This is the Word of God who came to his own people in the person of Jesus – according to the prologue of John's Gospel – yet his own people received him not. This is humanity expelling God in the person of Jesus, whereas we tend to think of God expelling humanity, or of God expelling Jesus. But no, we expel those we blame for humanity's problems and ultimately, we expel God by expelling Jesus. Jesus enters into this system to expose and undo it, not to confirm it or to perpetuate it. This expelling violence isn't how the world is meant to work anymore.

We get a foretaste of this transformation in our Old Testament texts tonight. In our Exodus reading, viewed through the spectacles that René Girard has given us, we can see how this Passover text points to a changed view of sacrifice.

First, it's lambs not people – just as the sacrifice of Abraham's son is replaced by the sacrifice of a sheep, so here the sacred writer points us away from the old order of human sacrifice. This is reinforced by the sacrifice de-emphasised in favour of simply eating the lambs, with a minimum of ritual – a further shift from the old sacrificial mindset. Next, God declares his judgment on the gods of Egypt. These are, of course, sacrificial deities, and their day is clearly done. We read that there will be a plague in Egypt and that God will strike down every firstborn child and animal. I suggest that what stands behind this confronting and perhaps opaque testimony is a social crisis, which is often represented in mythology as a plague – a plague that's typically resolved by animal and maybe human sacrifice, including perhaps sacrificing the firstborn, who are the most precious.

So here, I suggest, is a veiled picture of the old sacrificial religion, desperately grinding its way over victims to keep a lid on social disorder – to bring the plague, so called, to an end. As for God striking down the firstborn, this is typical Old Testament talk for saying simply that God allows it to happen, because God allows everything to happen. So, what's presented here as Israel's God taking life in punishment is really the description of an actual pagan outburst of targeted violence aimed at resolving a dire social crisis. Indeed, it's even been suggested that the escape of the Hebrews would have precipitated such a social crisis, just as freeing the slaves created a social crisis in the post-Civil War American South that the structural violence of Jim Crow sought to contain. Instead, God's deliverance of Israel from the plague and from death can be understood as God's call for a different kind of society, a different kind of sacrifice, and a different basis for human togetherness based on God's goodness, not on cathartic blame and condemnation.

This is why our Psalm tonight emphasises a new type of sacrifice, which it calls a sacrifice of thanksgiving. Following Jesus, in this spirit, we Christians thankfully give our lives to God, for the sake of a world that needs to see and learn a different way, and of course it's our responsibility to point that way. This is why Anglican Eucharistic liturgy describes itself as a sacrifice of praise and thanksgiving, in the words of our Psalm, and why at the end of our Eucharist, we're invited to see our self-offering to God as a living sacrifice. For some, the memory of violence attaches to these words, and understandably so, which is why alternative words for this liturgical dismissal are provided. But the truest insight here is that God dares to allow the old sacrificial language, and imagery, while turning it inside out. The self-sacrifice of God, given into our hands, is meant to upset the apple cart of human *realpolitik* and make a new world order possible – a new world order called Church, a new world order called Eucharist. And our way into this new world order involves joining Jesus in his self-offering, in his humble service. That way, we pass beyond hurt egos, self-justification, envy, rivalry, violence, payback, lynching and a catharsis that's only ever temporary. Instead of all this familiar business as usual, we have a new sacrifice, a world-transforming one. Jesus gives himself and we Christians respond Eucharistically, with our own sacrifice of praise and thanksgiving.

The Lord be with you …

A Tough and Genuine Alternative

Holy Thursday (Maundy Thursday), 29 March 2018,
St Philip's, O'Connor.

Exodus 12:1-14; Psalm 116; 1-2, 11-18;
1 Corinthians 11:23-26; John 13:1-17, 31b-35

✝ In the Name of the Father and of the Son and of the Holy Spirit. Amen.

Tonight, in our first gathering for the Easter Triduum, we begin to see how Jesus is changing the world. Tonight, we gather to witness and to unpack his radical action in offering his own body to be broken for us, and in the seemingly undignified and degrading action of washing his disciples' feet. And when I say action, I mean 'action' the way that activists mean it. But, friends, this isn't the familiar activism of angry one-upmanship and tit for tat. Rather, Jesus' activism of loving service and self-giving offers a shakeup that undercuts our ideologies and our rusted-on habits of mind, and surely this is what our world needs – a shakeup that you and I are encouraged to experience and then to join in. Jesus' new commandment tonight, that we love one another – this mandate, this *mandatum* – provides the name for this Maundy Thursday, and it sets the agenda for all the baptised to carry away from here tonight.

Now, it's too easy to blame the world of politics and politicians for failures of service and self-sacrifice. Indeed, it's typical of us that we neglect our own culpability in the world's business as usual and blame others. We like to assert our superiority, clinging to our advantages, feeling free to be envious and rivalrous and complicit in violence – even if all we contribute is our gossip, our invective, or our silence. We fear being outsiders, being disadvantaged and, ultimately, we fear losing everything through failure, decline and ultimately death. So, we look out for number one, we fear losing our precious distinctiveness, or else we try obsessively to fit in in case we end up exposed and alone. But, friends, in baptism and Eucharist we discover a new sense of who we are and of life's meaning, also in the wonderful addendum to the Last Supper that John's Gospel gives us tonight, when Jesus washes his disciple's feet. So, what's it all about?

First, the foot washing. This is all about refusing the siren song of rivalry, of ambition, of me and mine before you and yours, of you win I lose, of all the prudential wisdom that we still teach our children when we train and educate them for success. Jesus' radical action with his disciples is stunning. He knows that, because afterwards he asks them, "Do you know what I have done for you?" Jesus' action shows that it's not about being an insider, being a winner, and thereby somehow keeping at bay the fear of disadvantage and ultimately the fear of death. Instead, it's about discovering God's patient, non-intrusive, non-aggressive, change-making power, so our eyes come to dwell on God and the world God loves and not on our own main chance.

Now, it's important that we don't misunderstand and think that Jesus wants us to be servile. A lot of Christians labour under this misapprehension, and, unfortunately, some Christian women have been taught to think that service means being a doormat. Here, I'm struck by the exchange with Peter in the middle of tonight's gospel. Peter is very conscious of his smallness and of Jesus' greatness and so, at first, he refuses Jesus' washing of his feet. But when Jesus chides Peter that it's essential for Christians to be part of this, or else they can hardly be Christians at all, Peter the painfully self-conscious immediately corrects his mistake, insisting that Jesus go the whole hog, washing Peter's hands and head as well. But "No", says Jesus. "You're not filthy and unworthy, you're already clean, worthy and significant, and you mustn't forget it!"

Holy Thursday (Maundy Thursday)

Peter gets a firm reassurance of his Christian dignity – that the disciples are already caught up in Jesus' life, so that Jesus is justified in trusting them with this commission, this mandate, to go and do likewise. In other words, Jesus encourages Peter and us to think more confidently of ourselves as Christians, to claim our place by right alongside Jesus in God's loving mission to the world, to not think of ourselves as unworthy, to not assume that being God's agent, God's minister, is for other people but not for us. Yes, the mission is a humble, self-effacing one, but it requires a sense of our own dignity, our own purpose, to dare to step up and embrace it.

And speaking of daring, Jesus then undertakes the most radical action of all. In the Last Supper, which was already being carried on in the Church when Paul came along and handed on the tradition, as we hear in tonight's Epistle, Jesus gives himself entirely in the face of the world's evil – Jesus becomes food to sustain us as we go and do likewise.

Now, this self-offering by Jesus on the cross and in the Eucharist isn't about placating an angry God, with Jesus undergoing punishment in our place. Friends, *we're the punishers*, not God. The religious and political anxieties of the day, Jewish and Roman – anxieties that are still alive and well in our world and in our hearts today – are what punishes Jesus, because he calls the whole system into question.

We might be happy to talk about God if by God we mean what grounds and guarantees and preserves the system and represents the projection of our favourite prejudices. But what if God isn't effectively our own creation, confined to this familiar scripted role in support of the *status quo*? What if, instead, God is real, and unconventionally different? What if, instead, God invades the system in person in order to expose the system, bringing instead a whole new creation that runs on a whole different logic?

Friends, in this Maundy Thursday Eucharist, this Christian Passover, we don't see God's violence meted out against our enemies, as we saw in the old Passover account from our Exodus reading tonight. Instead, we see the whole impulse of human violence absorbed into God's own life in Jesus Christ, and taken responsibility for, and undone from the inside of history.

Popular notions of an aggressive, violent God only produce aggressive, violent human beings. But a God who undermines the *status quo* in the radical Eucharistic action of Jesus Christ, offering himself for the life of the world, opens a new world beyond violent self-justification, a world where unity and peace might at last have a chance.

Friends, where we prefer to tear apart those we blame for whichever set of problems, Jesus steps up and is himself torn apart – not to satisfy some pagan impulse or in tune with some ancient myth, but as a tough and genuine historical alternative to the whole inexorable grind of history. And friends, where can *today's* world look for that tough and genuine alternative? The most alarming news for us tonight, but also the most consoling, is that Jesus calls us, Jesus trusts us, to be signs of that tough and genuine alternative in the Church, and in our own lives.

The Lord be with you ...

Good Friday

Who is the Son of God?

Good Friday Sermon, 6 April 2007,
St Paul's, Manuka

† In the Name of the Father and of the Son and of the Holy Spirit. Amen.

Imagine if you will Imperial Rome in 46 BC, decked out for a triumph. Julius Caesar has subdued the Gallic tribes and Vercingetorix, his fierce former enemy, is displayed captive. If you saw the splendid recent TV series called *Rome*, this scene will have stayed in your memory. There is Caesar, played by Ciaron Hinds, his face painted red marking him as the son of God – as the figurehead of a divine Empire that required its leaders to be worshipped, like many other Empires before and since, even in some places to this day. And in front of the roaring crowd, Caesar's vanquished enemy, Vercingetorix, is garrotted. He's the scapegoat, the victim, on whom all can direct their anger and on whose death everyone can agree.

This is how Rome kept the peace – by violent suppression of dissent, certainly, but also by providing an endless retinue of scapegoats whose deaths united the population in festive unanimity. Hence the circus and the gladiators. Hence the triumphs and the ritual slaughter of enemies. Hence the positively Stalinist political intrigues, with the latest enemy of the state singled out for humiliation and death. And hence the daily scenes of crucifixion around the Roman Empire, like the one outside Jerusalem we remember today, where two thieves and a rabble-rouser went to their deaths, as signs that Roman power remained divine, and that everyone's best interests were served by proper submission.

In my mind's eye, I see the Centurion, mentioned in the Gospels, who led the troops sent out to handle these executions. I imagine him as a battle-hardened company commander who'd seen it all, done it all and caught it all – a seasoned soldier weary perhaps of fighting the Empire's battles far from home, and on this occasion trying to do a nasty job as efficiently and matter of factly as he could, eager to have Jesus' legs broken to hasten the end, so they could all get back to the barracks before the big weekend. Yet as the hours passed, this Centurion heard what Jesus said from the cross, and saw how he carried himself. Perhaps there's some poetic licence in the way the Gospels report it, portraying the Centurion as won over by Jesus in his death. Perhaps Christians suffering under the Roman Empire are meant to be encouraged by this Gospel – that if they suffer as Jesus did, their Roman persecutors will be converted, like the Centurion in the gospel.

But what strikes me is the link here to the Roman triumph, and the Son of God it honours, and the victim who dies a scapegoat. I like to think that this Centurion had been on parade in Rome for his share of triumphs and had picked out the red face of the divine son of god up above the crowd, giving the thumbs down on the shamed, defeated victim held captive down below. But somehow now, at the butt end of the Empire, older and wiser perhaps about the pretensions of emperors and great men, in the thick of it, amid all the blood and dust and the prolonged tragedy of lingering public death, the divinity of Rome was hard to see. And then, somehow, in this particular scapegoat, one of countless thousands, up and down the Empire, the Centurion senses an upset, a breakthrough, a new slant on the world, and what matters in it, and who God is, and who God isn't.

No longer does the face of the divine emperor, painted blood red, strike the Centurion as the face of God, but that other face, the bloody face of Jesus, mocked as King of the Jews, is now closer to the mark. Hence the Centurion's remarkable confession, 'Truly, this man was the son of God'. Truly in Christ the cosmic tables are turned and, as Yeats puts it, 'the ceremony of innocence is drowned'. This is what the judgment of God means, too, by the way, not a bloodbath rivalling anything Rome could conceive but, rather, the showing up of the big lie, including all the big religious lies that justify violence in the name of God.

And here's the heart of the gospel in a sentence. Not the false sacred realities that humans like to create – beautiful and terrible, violent and glorious – such as the Roman Empire, with its son of God in person as dispenser-in-chief of violent self-assurance. Rather, the self-effacing one who preferred the self-effacement of God to every human stratagem of self-promotion; the compassionate one who had no place for violence in his version of the sacred; the radically other-directed one, so sure of God's love and grace that he could go seeking it in the absence of beauty and goodness, in the depths of suffering and in absolute solidarity with the defeated ones of no account who don't register in the statistics of Empire.

The Centurion's confession means that in future, Rome is going to unravel, so that the violent *Pax Romana* won't work anymore. And so it was. The Kingdom of God, unleashed with power on the cross and confirmed as unstoppable in the resurrection, spoils it for all the false gods and proud Empires, so no-one can take them quite so seriously anymore. This Centurion was the first to experience Christ as the spirit of scepticism about proud, human-centred claims to have the divine all stitched up.

For us today, the confession of Jesus as Lord while he hangs on the cross is just as political a confession. It means we grant absolute authority to nothing else in the world – we never agree to follow any ideology uncritically, nor to worship at the throne of any political demagogue. This is the paradoxical triumph of the cross, mightier than any Roman triumph, and mighty reassuring when our own lives are anything but triumphant – when we find ourselves among the wretched of the earth, for instance, as victims and scapegoats ourselves, thanks to some grave mistake or misfortune.

Because we Christians know that this place of shame is now the dwelling place of God, and that it's a habitable place, since Jesus went there before us. The resurrection is the sign and seal of God on all this – not that Jesus is taken out of the realm of suffering and made like the mighty Roman emperor, ready now to dish out payback. Anything but. The risen Christ carries his wounds on his body, and his life thereafter at the heart of God is marked forever by the suffering solidarity he showed in his life and his death.

Truly this man was the son of God. Truly Jesus is Lord: not Caesar, not Stalin, not Hitler, not the global economy, not the honour code of tribe or crime family, not the path of stifling convention nor that of easy popularity. Today, on Good Friday, we encounter the only true God there is, setting the false gods aside, as Christ continues to win hearts among all who've had their fill of tired, pretentious nonsense – like that Centurion and, please God, like you and me too.

The Lord be with you...

At-one-ment Beyond Divine Violence

Good Friday, 25 March 2016,
All Saints', Ainslie.

† In the Name of the Father and of the Son and of the Holy Spirit. Amen.

People today often view the idea of sin ironically – in terms of transgressing trivial rules, and hence as a bit of a joke. Yet Christian tradition has always taken sin seriously as a universal condition. Sin is best described as a fundamental distortion of our humanity in which all of us are implicated, even when we're not aware of it. We Anglicans confess our sins collectively in every Sunday Eucharist, which is a singular thing for any community to do, when you think about it, and we keep the penitential seasons of Lent and Advent – Lent as a penitential season in the key of hope, and Advent as a hopeful season in the key of penitence. Yet even here the sense of our immersion in sin may not go very deep. In Lent and Advent, we might have a vague sense of being too caught up in consumerism, too attached to our own comforts, too distracted from the things of God, too insensitive to the needs of others, too lacking in compassion. But any recognition of being trapped in what amounts to an addiction that distorts and poisons us – our relationships, our society and our world – is a rather stronger diagnosis of our ills than we're accustomed to.

Indeed, the whole reality of being caught up in sin usually escapes us until we begin to get free of sin, to see beyond it, to recognise an alternative. Let me give some examples. Someone who's grown used to being abused and taken advantage of can lack a clear awareness of their plight until they find themselves freed from abuse, and in the hands of people who care for them. Or consider the abuser themselves, who often underestimates the harm they're doing until they get help to unpack their anger or their lust and come to understand its causes.

It's often only with hindsight and with added maturity that we can look back on our own lives and appreciate how much we've contributed to our own bad luck by the choices we've made, where once we might have blamed anybody but ourselves. Sometimes it's enough to meet a saint, who reveals God's gaze to us – a gaze of acceptance, but which misses nothing. This iconic gaze is an experience of judgment wrapped in forgiveness, which sets us on the road to conversion. As James Alison teaches, it's when we slowly begin to leave sinful mindsets and habits behind that we begin to recognise what actually had hold of us, what we used to be like, and what we were missing. This is equally true of us whether we belong to Islamic State or to the parish ladies' guild.

In our days there's so much refusal of accountability – from politicians, business leaders, and from purveyors of death and disease, with so many institutions and ordinary people going to any lengths to avoid responsibility. Accountability is not the characteristic virtue of our times. As I've been indicating, even in Christian circles, the reality of our sin can elude us, leading to a prideful refusal on our part to take responsibility and make amends. But the Bible and the Christian tradition are not deceived.

Of course, we shouldn't overdo the claims of sin, as if evil is ultimate and foundational in our world. As the creation myths of Babylon began with primal violence, so our book of Genesis responds with a picture of primal peace in creation: between humanity and God, humanity and the animals, and between husband and wife. The envy towards God, the rivalry, the duplicity and the violence came later, as the world took on more familiar lineaments in the Genesis story, as we came to see God as our rival, and as we opted for exile from God's presence – which, of course, we blamed on God, as we see in Genesis. The Bible's story begins with God's peace and goodness, not with human sin and violence, but that's never been our preference, has it?

Yet the God of the Bible is not content with leaving us to our own devices. For every Old Testament story of harsh legal demands and violent retribution against God's enemies – because this is how we humans like to think about God – there's a different story of God's patient work across the generations and through the prophets, that allows us to imagine a different sort of God, untainted by the habits of violent self-assertion and righteous payback that we humans prefer – from our political debates to our play-stations, and in many places even from our pulpits.

The reconciling high point for Christians is the person of Jesus Christ, who we know as God with us, revealing both God's outreach and our response in perfect accord, so that in Jesus' life, death and resurrection, our own life and death are transformed. At the heart of what the New Testament and the Creeds confess is that in Jesus Christ, God has dealt with human sin and broken its hold on us, forgiving us and transforming us so that we no longer need to be addicts but can be free people, rightly knowing ourselves, others, and God. The question, of course, is: how does this happen, this reconciliation that Jesus brings, fulfilling the good news of Hebrew Scripture, our Old Testament?

And here things can get tricky. This is because the message of how God and humanity have become at one in Jesus Christ – how there's been an at-one-ment, an atonement, between God and humanity through Jesus Christ – is sometimes explained in ways that can undo the good news that we seek to proclaim.

If many Anglicans have trouble with the idea of sin, let alone being trapped in sin, the proposed cure for sin can seem even more inexplicable. The Church has insisted that serious measures were needed, with Jesus' death playing a crucial and necessary role in turning the tide for sinful human beings with God. But this bedrock Christian conviction has been articulated in ways that seem impossible for us to reconcile with what we see of God in the Gospels and in light of the problems with violence that we struggle with today.

Anselm of Canterbury in the eleventh century articulated one important stream of Christian thought from antiquity. God's created order was distorted by human sin and had to be restored, but it wasn't fitting for God to impose a solution, because humans were the ones who had to make amends – yet how could sinful humans achieve that? So, a sinless human stepped in, Jesus the son of God, paying the ultimate price for an ultimate transgression, standing in for the rest of us as our substitute. With sixteenth-century Protestant Reformed theology, the emphasis shifted from substitution to punishment, with Jesus punished by God for our sins. There are passages in the Bible that support the idea of God needing Jesus to embrace the cross, but it's harder to find passages that see the cross in terms of God actually punishing Jesus in our place.

In the tradition of Calvin and the Puritans, however, through to the hard line of one major strand in Anglican Evangelicalism today, the good news about Christianity is chiefly this: that Jesus took a bullet for us, a bullet fired by an angry God, as our only way to recover the peace with God that we'd lost because of our sins. This is a message that no doubt brings comfort and relief to many Christians: those especially troubled by guilt, perhaps, or, worse, by shame. But those who hold tight to this so-called penal substitutionary view of the atonement need to realise that for others it represents an insurmountable obstacle.

Penal substitution – this idea that God punishes Jesus in our place – is a view of the atonement that many people in the modern West find unacceptable because of the Bible's apparent testimony to God's love and forgiveness, which comes with no strings attached.

Must there be such a sting in the tail? Must every abusive person be offered what strikes many feminists and others as a divine model for abusive behaviour? Hardline Evangelicals say that expressing penal substitution as I'm doing here is a caricature, that God's love is real but costly, and that Jesus had to pay the price of that love. But, for many of us, any subtlety here escapes us. At best this penal substitutionary view of the atonement is an impersonal transaction, and at worst it's been called "divine child abuse". If this is Christianity, many people today would prefer Enlightenment tolerance and some decent, non-judgmental secular pluralism, thank you very much. This is what many basically decent and thoughtful people have concluded and have left the Church accordingly. Anselm on satisfaction and substitution, through to Calvin and the Puritans on divine punishment in our place, suggest a God who uses violence to restore peace and order – this is Mel Gibson's God, but is it the God of Jesus Christ?

And is it a God who takes seriously the deep-rooted nature of sin as I've described it? If we've become aware of sin in ourselves and among ourselves, we probably recognise that letting go of it is a process of growing self-awareness and slow personal transformation, not simply a once-for-all transaction. Our at-one-ment with God is a journey, in which our minds and hearts change over time to embrace something new. Conversion isn't instantaneous, once we acknowledge Jesus as our saviour. Another medieval writer, Peter Abelard, put the emphasis in atonement on this process of human transformation. The atonement takes place subjectively in our hearts as the reality of God's loving solidarity through Jesus' sinless suffering on the cross begins to soften and to change our hearts.

Where many, and especially Anselm, have insisted that atonement is *objective*, involving a transaction between God the Father and Jesus on our behalf, Abelard offers a *subjective* version, focused on how Jesus' sacrifice affects us and changes us. And it's certainly true that this subjective component is important. As we look at Jesus crucified, as we go forward to the foot of the cross on Good Friday, it's this movement of love that we feel from God, and that we're moved to return as we sing, "Love so amazing, so divine, demands my soul, my life, my all".

Yet is it enough to move the heart in order to change the world? Is the work of the cross sufficient if it's confined to the realm of personal piety? All those who cry out to a silent God in the face of history's horrors, all those victims of murder and savagery who plead for their lives to no avail, rightly yearn for a more powerful sign from God, a surer justice, and a stronger medicine for the stubborn evils that bedevil human history. Can we acknowledge the subjective dimension of the atonement while keeping its objectivity, and discover the power of God in the powerlessness of Jesus' cross? Can the cross be the liberating judgment of God at the same time as it works the softening and yielding of our own hardened hearts?

The answer of course is 'yes'. A world of sin is confronted by the sinless one, who meets violence with non-violence, curses with forgiveness, and the fear of death wielded as the ultimate weapon with a willingness to die that disempowers that fear. Seeing Jesus' cross as a victory in which we come to share combines the cross's objective impact with its subjective force. So, it's not about Jesus paying a price to God for our disobedience or being punished by God in our place. Indeed, it's not about a violent God at all, because all the violence in the passion of Jesus Christ comes from human beings.

But it is a willing sacrifice of a certain sort that Jesus offers, without which the Church has never believed that sin can be overcome. And, of course, Jesus' resurrection is the great sign of this victory made complete. The risen Jesus Christ is revealed from heaven, as Archbishop Peter Carnley liked to point out – revealed as humanly alive yet at one with God, so that Christians are caught up mystically with him by the Holy Spirit into a new life and a new future as the Church of the risen Jesus Christ.

This is the vision of our reconciliation with God that I want to commend to you today, beyond the versions of atonement that can't tell the whole story and that risk distorting the good news they seek to proclaim. In particular, I want to see Jesus' death at human hands as at the same time God's saving act on our behalf that changes everything, as the resurrection reveals. Yet I want to make this claim in a consistent way, holding together all that the New Testament declares about the God of love, about the power of powerlessness, and about the force of love being greater than violence. This is what the cross of Jesus reveals, and this is what his suffering means – not paying off an angry God, but changing the world for angry people, so that God can get through to them, and them to God.

The Lord be with you...

Good Friday: *Alone in Berlin*

Good Friday, 14 April 2017,
St James', King Street, Sydney.

Isaiah 52:13-53:12, Psalm 22, I Corinthians 1:18-31, John 18:1 to 19:42

† In the Name of the Father and of the Son and of the Holy Spirit. Amen.

> So he shall startle many nations;
> Kings shall shut their mouths because of him;
> for that which had not been told them they shall see,
> and that which they had not heard they shall contemplate.
> Who has believed what we have heard?
> And to whom has the arm of the Lord been revealed?
> (Isaiah 52:13 to 53:1)

At the cinema recently, you may have seen a fine film with Brendan Gleeson and Emma Thompson in the leading roles, called *Alone in Berlin*. It's based on the novel by Hans Fallada, but in turn on real events from the early 1940s, about an ordinary German couple's simple but profound act of resistance against the Nazi terror. On Good Friday, when we celebrate God's great act of resistance against humanity's violent, godless business as usual, this film provides an apt illustration of what it is that we celebrate today.

Otto and Anna Quangel were brother and sister, but in the film they were portrayed as a married couple who'd lost their son killed in action. This helped convince them that the Nazi war machine was in fact a great evil and that their mission in life was to oppose it. What they then did was place messages of protest all over Berlin on postcards – in doorways and stairwells, in public places, hundreds of cards, all carefully written to disguise the handwriting. The messages denounced a murderous regime, exposing the lie that Nazism was all for Germany and all for the good. But theirs was a dangerous game, at a time when party spies reported on the residents of apartment buildings, neighbourhoods and workplaces – like the factory that Otto ran, making ever greater numbers of coffins for dead German soldiers.

The Berlin police and the Gestapo were alarmed by this non-violent protest. Tyrannous regimes never like the truth being spoken, and their power being mocked, so these offenders had to be caught. What the film doesn't show, but the book does, is just how terrified and conflicted people were to find Otto's cards, in case they were implicated. Because everyone becomes complicit in a terror state, at least to some extent, where an open mind and a generous spirit can get you into trouble.

Eventually, as you might imagine, Otto and Anna were caught, tried, and executed – in their case, to ramp up the terror, they were beheaded. They knew what they were doing, and the risks. I was struck by the way that Otto Quangel faced his accusers and his ordeal with a degree of confident, superior detachment. So it was for Jesus, in John's Gospel today, as the official national religion and the Roman terror state turned their full force against him. Yet, in John's Gospel, Jesus isn't afraid. He interrogates the Roman procurator, not vice versa; he carries his own cross; he brings the faithful forever under the protection of his own mother, and vice versa, in the scene with John and Mary and, when he's good and ready, he announces "It is finished".

We also see in John's Gospel that Pilate recognises Jesus' innocence and wants to help him. So, too, in the film, Escherich, the Berlin police detective (played by Daniel Brühl), who eventually catches the Quangels, experiences remorse. He waits for Otto on his final lonely walk to the guillotine and asks almost apologetically if he can do anything for him. Otto looks him in the face and then replies, "give me a card and pen". There's no easy forgiveness here;

the enormity of the evil remains and can't be denied or smoothed over. The only answer is to oppose it and, when overpowered by it, not to give in.

We see Peter giving in in today's Gospel. He just wanted to be one of the crowd. "I'm not Jesus' disciple", he declared. Earlier, in the garden, when Jesus was arrested, Peter had already let himself be sucked in by the mob when he struck out with his sword in reciprocal violence, cutting off someone's ear. Instead, Jesus in John's Gospel, like Otto Quangel from *Alone in Berlin*, lives and dies in a way that doesn't perpetuate violence and, in this way, denies the system its victory – a system that never got the better of him. And when someone manages to turn the tables in this way, others notice, and are empowered to do the same.

In the film, however, Escherich the detective isn't one of these. He can't live with what he's done, so he throws hundreds of Otto's confiscated cards out the window of his office in Police Headquarters, so people in the square below could pick them up and get the message, then he shoots himself. The suicide of Judas was probably similar, once he'd realised the terrible mistake that he'd made. How much better it would have been if Judas in the Bible and the German policeman Escherich in the film hadn't accepted defeat at the hands of the system, finally acquiescing in self-destruction.

Friends, on Good Friday we see the truth that Pilate can't admit. When he asks his question "What is truth"?, he shows that he's prepared to assent to anything – that it suits him to fit in, to take refuge in 'alternative facts'. And on Good Friday we see that the mob always prefers someone like Barabbas, who fits into the system. He's the enemy who reveals that we're all friends. We can't do without Barabbas, or his fellow terrorists today, just as we can't apparently do without having asylum seekers whom we refuse to welcome – because without them who would we be, we sane and normal and right-thinking people who belong here? What we don't want is someone like Jesus, or Otto Quangel for that matter, who shows up the system and who calls it into question. Instead, on

Good Friday, we see God's shocking alternative to this way that the world works. We see the lies revealed, the threats faced and not given in to, the mechanism of blame-shifting and scapegoating exposed, and the underlying logic of death brought to light.

In John's Gospel account of the passion, Jesus resists being overcome by all this. He isn't caught up in the system, as Peter is, along with Pilate, the chief priests, and the Roman soldiers. Otto Quangel does the same. And so can you, so can I, as we enter into Jesus' alternative imagination, ignoring with him the siren song of belonging that so entranced Peter. Because, friends, if we belong to God, we can never be entirely at ease in the world, never comfortably ensconced on the left or the right, or indeed anywhere in the system.

This is why the servant of Yahweh in our Isaiah reading today, with whose words I began, represents such a startling challenge to the nations, to kings, to the powers that be, to the status quo. This is why our Psalmist today begins with the weight of the system crushing him but ends with a lightness and a freedom born of hope. So too can we can face our end, knowing that Jesus has walked this path before us and has come back from the worst our world can offer – thanks to God, to Easter.

And, friends, this is why St Paul in our 1 Corinthians reading today describes the cross as a scandal to Jews and as foolishness to Gentiles, to Greeks, because the message of the cross isn't sustainable according to typical religious or philosophical standards. It's not the familiar logic of payback, of self-assertion at the expense of others. But nor is it simply about giving up in disgust at the system and disgust at ourselves – as Judas did, and the Berlin detective Escherich, too, ultimately absorbed and defeated by the system. Instead, Jesus took it on, while not giving into it and becoming like it as Peter did. In this way, Jesus' cross absorbs the evil of the system, pointing beyond its sterile options, resetting human life beyond self-defining conflict. And with the confirmation that comes on Easter Sunday, a new resurrection spirit is unleashed in the world, beyond the power of death, beyond every constraint of the system.

So, the cross is indispensable if we're to understand God, to free our imaginations, to find true human freedom, and to picture genuine social alternatives. The cross is the act that sets us free from sin, on our way to claiming that freedom on Easter Day, at Pentecost, and whenever we celebrate the Christian saints. Friends, the cross is not an Aztec-style sacrifice to preserve the status quo, to pacify an angry God, to restore a deformed world by performing the right ritual, though it certainly does evoke comparisons with all that. Instead, it's the destruction of that stable, comfortable world, and it's God's invitation to do the world in new ways – through the adventure of faith, through the adventure of Church, through the adventure of being a Eucharistic community.

That way, the cross also becomes the pattern of a new kind of human life that we can embrace. Beyond looking out for number one, beyond me and mine versus you and yours, beyond leave well alone, beyond everything that St Paul calls the wisdom of this world, God's alternative wisdom revealed by the cross offers us new conditions, a new start, and a new identity. Any other solution would simply have left everything as it was. Otto Quangel knew this reality, alone in Berlin, yet not alone as he overcame the stifling conformity, the numbing fear of being alone, and the dread of death, which is the fuel on which this whole system runs. Jesus went through all this, and beyond it. So did Otto Quangel – and so can we, you and me.

The Lord be with you ...

Easter Day
(First Sunday of Easter)

The Resurrection Includes Us

Easter Day, 16 April 2017, Year A,
St James', King Street, Sydney

Acts 10:34-43; Hymn to the Risen Christ;[4]
Colossians 3:1-4; Matthew 28:1-10

☩ In the Name of the Father and of the Son and of the Holy Spirit. Amen.

> Set your minds on things that are above, not on things that are on earth, for you have died, and your life is hidden with Christ in God. (Colossians 3:3)

Friends, this is a very strong statement, and nothing I encountered in the nominal Anglican home of my childhood would have helped me to comprehend it. This powerful declaration from Colossians today actually explains the meaning and content of my baptism as an infant, though, of course, that event would have been understood as a social obligation in accord with bourgeois respectability rather than a radical rebirth to a new identity and a new agenda for living. Indeed, the very idea that there was anything wrong with us, and with our suburban life and its standard priorities – such that our minds had to be lifted up and out of that world, such that in some sense we had to die to that world – would have made no sense at all.

This was a world, after all, where respectable Protestant householders and taxpayers didn't have to worry about things like sin, which was something that nice people weren't involved in. As for setting our minds on things above, that could only mean a

---

4 See Appendix

look of pious composure, to accompany appearances in our Sunday best. The notion of being trapped in sin, of being addicted to a proud self-sufficiency, wouldn't have been an explicable let alone an acceptable diagnosis, according to the wisdom of that world – a world in which there wasn't much genuine openness to others, in which God marked the remote edges of life but did not occupy its centre, in which Jesus was never named, in which the word "God" was an optional addition in commending a safe, prudential morality.

But, friends, that's not the world of Easter, it's not the point of our Eucharist today, it's not the logic of our readings, and it's not the meaning of our Christian lives. The temperature is higher today, the mood far more expectant, the joy not quite containable, and if it isn't, then I don't quite know what we think we're doing here today. Does Easter just mean that every cloud has a silver lining, or that there's a heaven for all good children beyond the bright blue sky? Or does the eruption of Jesus Christ from the throttling of death and defeat to remake the world in the power of his resurrection actually burst the bounds of flat, conventional, self-regarding, semi-Christian morality and threaten instead to blow our minds, to set them on something above – above business as usual, above predictable piety?

Friends, in our readings today, the resurrection reaches out to grasp us and transform us. It happened 2000 years ago, and it happens today. The resurrection involves us – our hearts, our imaginations, our minds, our changed lives – and is given liturgical expression in the Eucharist. We see it in all our readings.

In Acts today, we see minds lifted up to a new way of doing the world. Jews and gentiles together find themselves drawn into a new experience of forgiveness, of energy unleashed, of mission embraced, of a world transformed in light of the risen Christ. What a contrast with many parts of our Church, where the very thought of mission and evangelism seems worse than a trip to the dentist.

Easter Day (First Sunday of Easter)

But here's the reality of Easter: people swept up with Christ into a new agenda, a new adventure, a new *raison d'être*.

This is an image that we also hear in the Easter Anthems this morning, the hymn to the risen Christ: the Church is invited to see itself as dead to sin but alive to God in Jesus Christ. All the things that we do and don't do as individuals, families, and as a Church, things that diminish and damage ourselves, others and the world, are put on notice today. We don't have to sigh reluctantly about our powerlessness in the face of them or put them out of our minds. Instead, we can consider ourselves dead to all that, as part of Jesus Christ – not perfect, to be sure, but not condemned to stubborn and toxic imperfection either. This is the imagery of baptism: we die with Adam, drowned in the font, then we rise with Christ, swimming in his new life like dolphins, rejoicing in our freedom.

This is the life that Colossians imagines for us today: looking to where Christ now sits at the right hand of God, in the place of honour. In my upbringing, no one talked about Jesus and, if asked, probably wouldn't know what to say, except perhaps that he expects children to be nice. Yet beyond the role of teacher, or as some vague pointer to prudential wisdom, Colossians today imagines Jesus at the heart of who God is and what God means. Looking to Jesus lifted up in glory isn't to condemn the non-Christian religions to ignominy, or to become religious weirdos ourselves, but to become like Jesus. And if the Church becomes more like Jesus, and ourselves, too, then the world has nothing to fear, then progressive agendas have nothing to fear, then honest searchers after God in whatever religious tradition have nothing to fear, and nor do honest atheists have anything to fear, because Jesus as God for us means that we are *for* the world, *for* the cause of life and liberty, *for* the sharing of joy and the sharing of God, with no hatred or superiority.

Finally, in our Gospel today, which was also read for the Easter Vigil at dawn this morning, we again see that resurrection is a collective reality. Its centre is Jesus' dead body and the events of

2000 years ago, but its circumference includes our world today, ourselves, and our future. Nobody in the New Testament simply observes the risen Jesus and remains unmoved. Here in the Gospel, the sight of Jesus evokes the worship of the women and sends them out on a mission from God to begin proclaiming the risen Christ.

Friends, this mission is also something we have a part in – we who are baptised, who share in the Eucharist, and who have a sense of being caught up in all this. Though I'm sure that not everyone has that sense here today. I say this not as a criticism, but to highlight a possibility, and to issue an invitation. Many yearn to be part of something bigger than themselves, and may have tried various options, hopefully with some success, though success isn't always the outcome. But here, friends, we're encountering something bigger than ourselves that can transform and resituate our lives, beyond prudential wisdom, beyond lukewarm or half-digested faith, beyond it all being a big unfathomable mystery, and perhaps beyond all the dead ends that we keep running into.

I conclude with a warning – that Easter isn't a happy pill. Jesus offers us no escape from having to live in the real world. But beyond the imaginative hold that death exerts, beyond the widespread agenda of self-preservation, likewise beyond the corresponding turn to recklessness and risk that helps others shake themselves free from the fear of death, and beyond the widespread agenda of getting what we can in a competitive game of life, there is an alternative. Instead, we can set our minds on things above, where Christ is, and where our baptism and Eucharist take us.

I hope that if your heart is so moved today you can rejoice in this Easter Eucharist, and then perhaps seek out the parish clergy to begin exploring what God might have in store for you. And whatever that might be, you can be sure it won't be dull, respectable, half-hearted Christianity. It will be edgier, more engrossing, more frustrating, and a lot more fun than that.

The Lord be with you ...

Caught up in the New Creation

Easter Day, 1 April 2018, Year B,
St Philip's, O'Connor.

Acts 10:34-43; Psalm 118:1-2, 14-24;
1 Corinthians 15:1-11; John 20:1-18

† In the Name of the Father and of the Son and of the Holy Spirit. Amen.

The stone that the builders rejected:
   has become the head of the corner.
This is the Lord's doing:
   and it is marvellous in our eyes. (Psalm 118:22-23)

These words from today's Psalm are used by Christians to proclaim the glory of Easter. On the one side, there had been religion and politics and cynical pragmatism, and the whole satanic mechanism that keeps order and control through exclusion and force; on the other side, there was a vulnerable and loving man sent by a vulnerable and loving God, who faced up to the world's worst terrors and tortures while refusing to perpetuate the cycle of violence. Jesus was that stone rejected by the builders of our conventional, more-or-less functional way of doing things and, like all of his kind, he had to be gotten rid of. Yet something happened following Jesus' death that galvanised a new hope among his traumatised followers.

It appeared that God had vindicated the dead Jesus, who was back among his people. Jesus risen was the same yet wonderfully different, having gone ahead of us into the life of God. No wonder Christians quickly concluded that in Jesus Christ, God had visited his people to set them free, and hence that Jesus was one with God, the human face of God, the Son of God, as they started to say, who reveals the glory of his Father. All the New Testament writers and, later, the creeds with their doctrines of incarnation and Trinity, testified to our growing appreciation of who Jesus was, and what sort of breakthrough he'd opened up, and who we've become, thanks to his resurrection and his Spirit dwelling among us.

So, when we hear our readings this morning, we're hearing voices from the early Church explaining what they were discovering about this new living reality, and about its implications. They didn't just proclaim a wonder from the past. Nor did anyone in the early Church think of the resurrection as a simple matter of belief, without it having any impact on how we live now. Instead, what we see in the New Testament is that encountering the risen Jesus was at the same time a summons to conversion and faith and mission – to be drawn into a wonderful thing that wasn't just in the past, but which was now and forever.

The earliest New Testament voice in our readings this morning is that of Paul. He tells the Corinthian Christians that the resurrection tradition, which had been handed on to him from the first Christian generation, was something that he was handing on to them, something in which they stood now – in other words, not something to look back on, but something to actually be part of. Paul laments that he'd effectively been one of those builders who'd rejected Jesus, by rejecting and persecuting the Church, but thanks to his own late encounter with the resurrection, Paul came to realise that God had made Jesus the very cornerstone. Amazed by grace, Paul saw himself as living proof of the reality of Jesus' resurrection.

So did Peter, our next oldest Easter witness this morning, channelled for us by Luke in our reading from Acts. Peter speaks as head of the Church in Jerusalem, explaining how Jesus had helped the apostles to reinterpret Israel's national story, catching them up into his risen life as witnesses to a new reality of forgiveness not judgment, of humanity reunited with God. This new reality requires apostolic witnesses like Peter and the others – right through to our bishops today, as the apostolic succession is handed down the generations. So friends, the origin of Easter is certainly way back then, but the life of Easter is here and now, as is the challenge to our generation of constantly rediscovering it, living it, and handing it on.

Then, from late in the first century, comes our resurrection testimony today from John's Gospel. This isn't like a police report that states plain, uninterpreted facts. Rather, it's a late document, and its aim is to draw out implications of the resurrection for the Church. Let me briefly mention three aspects of this – of what life in the resurrection meant for the Christians among whom John's Gospel took shape.

First, in today's Gospel, did you notice the foot race to the empty tomb on Easter morning? Peter and the beloved disciple are neck and neck, this pair who always seem at odds in John's gospel – Peter the great apostle, and whoever the beloved disciple is (perhaps the Christian everyman, as Fr Martin suggested in his reflection here on Good Friday). Did you notice that the beloved disciple wins the race, but that Peter is the first to enter the tomb, but then Peter couldn't work it out, while the beloved disciple does work it out and becomes the first to believe?

What we seem to have here is an early recognition among Christians that leadership in the Church has two dimensions, which Leonardo Boff called charism and power. Peter represents power and authority, while the beloved disciple represents spirituality and personal closeness to Jesus. Are we being told here that we need both: that we need popes and we need saints, that we need bishops and we need theologians, that we need priests and we need laity, and that the tension along all these axes is actually a creative tension that helps us know and serve the risen Christ better? This arrangement brings a kind of hybrid vigour that you don't get in the type of Church that's all about centralised power, or in the type of Church that's all about decentralised spirituality. Our

Anglican tradition is committed to maintaining this tension. We're a traditional episcopal Church yet we have a dispersed form of governance with a place of dignity for everyone – or at least that's the theory. We Anglicans seek to maintain the creative centre where Catholic and Orthodox and Protestant emphases can meet. This is the type of Church in which God calls us to experience and to hand on the resurrection life.

Second, in today's Gospel from John, there's the Old Testament imagery that Mary Magdalene experiences. As she looked into the empty tomb, she was carried back to the Holy of Holies in the Jerusalem Temple, with the cherubim on either side of the ark of the covenant, which was empty. The two angels at either end of where Jesus' body had lain recall that holiest of sites among God's people – a place now occupied by the risen Jesus Christ.

Then follows her scene in the Garden, and, of course, we're meant to think of the Garden of Eden. But when the voice of Jesus comes to Mary Magdalene, just as the voice of God came to Eve in the Genesis story, Mary Magdalene is not disobedient. Hence, in this new Garden of Eden, we see creation beginning again. Just as Jesus the new Adam did not disobey God in the Garden of Gethsemane, Mary Magdalene as a new Eve did not betray God in this Easter Garden.

My third point here is that all bets are clearly off for John's Gospel in its account of the resurrection. Not only could a woman look into the Holy of Holies, but a woman could now be commissioned as an apostle, sent to proclaim the good news to men, at a time when women couldn't even be witnesses under Jewish law. So, Eve's curse has been lifted, and a woman leads humanity into a new age.

Certainly, this story of Mary Magdalen, the so-called apostle to the apostles, was one of the texts that helped a legislative majority in our Church's General Synod to embrace the idea that women could and should be priests and bishops. Because Jesus' resurrection means that the aeons are shifting, so that the world is beginning again for us in new and unexpected ways.

To sum up: the old way of building the world, which involved Jesus being got rid of, is suddenly revealed to have got things completely wrong. Instead, the stone that the builders rejected has become the cornerstone.

For Paul, the former persecutor of Christianity, the risen Jesus Christ summoned him into a new life, to a new self-understanding. For Peter, another who'd denied Jesus, the resurrection brought a new start and a new life beyond failure and judgment – a faith being handed on from the first witnesses to new witnesses in every generation. For John's Gospel today, the resurrection brought a new way of being together which is hybrid and creative. Finally, in company with Mary Magdalene, we find ourselves in the Holy of Holies, and returned to the Garden of Eden with a second chance.

So, friends, on Easter Day we don't just acknowledge an unlikely past event and then go home to our lives in the real world. Instead, here in the Eucharist for Easter Day, we discover a *more real world* – the very world into which we've already been inducted through our baptism.

This is the day that the Lord has made:
Let us rejoice and be glad in it. (Psalm 118:24)

The Lord be with you ...

The Resurrection: But What about the Eggs?

Easter Day, 4 April 2021, Year B,
St Philip's, O'Connor.

Isaiah 25:6-9; Hymn to the Risen Christ;[5]
Acts 10:34-43; Mark 16:1-8

✝ In the Name of the Father and of the Son and of the Holy Spirit. Amen.

There's a tradition that sermons on Easter Day should begin with a joke, because the resurrection invites us to laugh in the face of so many fears that people take way too seriously, not least the fear of death. So here goes. In Woody Allen's film *Annie Hall*, we're told about a man who asked a psychiatrist about his brother, who thought he was a chicken. The psychiatrist said to bring the brother along so he could be cured. The man replied, "but we need the eggs".

Friends, the resurrection of Jesus Christ reminds me of this joke – that something so unlikely might actually be the case, if we look at the bigger picture. So, let's do that, starting with the earliest and least elaborate of the resurrection stories in all our four gospels, the one from Mark, which we heard this morning.

It's a story of confusion, encounter, promise, then more confusion. There's no appearance from Jesus, only an empty tomb and that inconclusive meeting with a witness, whoever that might be. The promise is that if Jesus' disciples and Peter their leader go to

---

5 See Appendix

Galilee, if they go out to the wider world, then the risen Jesus will reveal himself among them, just as he'd told them. In other words, the proof of the resurrection pudding will be in the missional eating. Going out in Jesus' name will turn out to involve encounters with Jesus. This resurrection story is so minimal that a second ending was added to Mark's Gospel subsequently, to beef the story up a bit. Maybe this earlier ending wasn't thought to be definite enough, and perhaps even a bit embarrassing.

But for today's world that typically struggles with religious truth claims, the idea that resurrection isn't meant to be obvious or in your face and can only commend itself through the life of faith might gain some fresh traction. Scientifically-minded people resist the idea that anything can intrude on the closed world of empirical evidence and rational necessity. Humanities-minded people affirm a world of different stories and perspectives without expecting any of them to represent absolute truth – as Don Cupitt once wrote, every timeless truth is a period piece. But the claim that Jesus is alive from God and that Christians come to know him in the life of faith is truth of a different order, neither purely subjective or relative on the one hand, nor provable by observation or rational necessity on the other.

Let me briefly mention two other points from our readings today. Our Hymn to the Risen Christ is about the meaning of Jesus' resurrection and not primarily its naked facticity. Jesus' resurrection is the cause of celebration, feasting, joy, and a new imperative to live beyond the power of sin – to experience a new aliveness that still holds up against today's widespread alternatives, where shame and trauma and crises of identity rob so many of peace and even of sanity. Finding a new lease of life is at the heart of what resurrection belief means for Christians, and without one we can't typically make sense of the other. Resurrection believing and finding a Resurrection spring in your step are two sides of the one coin. The joy of today's Isaiah passage, from the Old Testament, reveals a hopeful religious imagination on the lookout for such new beginnings. Christians found this new beginning in the Church's shared experience, with a sense that Jesus was alive from God in the Eucharist they celebrated and the lives they lived as a faith community.

This is what we see in our Acts reading today, with Peter's sermon giving us a window into what the earliest Christian preaching entailed. The witnesses to Jesus' ministry and his death on the cross also testified in various ways to their sense that he was alive with them, some very explicitly. But Peter chiefly testifies to new breakthrough insights that were galvanising the earliest Churches – in this case, to the new influx of non-Jewish people who were pressing their claim on the Church, which Peter sees as a new world-transforming reality announcing itself.

And it's worth noting here that this isn't how resurrections present themselves elsewhere in world mythology. Resurrections in mythology often involve a persecuted figure back from the dead to re-knit a persecuted group, confirming the group's partiality over against a hostile environment. But not this resurrection. Peter declares that God shows no partiality – *no partiality* – as the Church's boundaries are opened wide to the other, not drawn tight against it.

Friends, in all these ways, the resurrection of Jesus Christ presents itself as a new, subtle, inclusive energy in the lives of Christians linked to Jesus' presence and that of his body, though in a variety of ways. Peter in Acts declares that many had testified to meeting the risen Jesus. But then don't forget Mark's rather different early account. There we find an empty tomb and a sense that something remarkable is afoot though there's no objective meeting with the risen Jesus, but only the promise that he'd meet his followers on the road.

So, back to my Woody Allen story. While it's odd that someone might think they're a chicken, the eggs do demand an explanation. Likewise, with the resurrection, which from the start was a way of interpreting Jesus' impact, and the Church's sense of his continuing presence – that for Christians, Jesus is a living Lord rather than a dead founder. This isn't meant to be nailed down cognitively or to compete with what today's sciences and humanities can teach us. Instead, it involves a more integral, a more allusive, a more participatory sort of knowing. Yes, it's weird, but then what about the eggs?

The Lord be with you ...

Ascension

In Heart and Mind there Ascend

Ascension Day, 20 May 2004, Year C,
St Paul's, Manuka.

Acts 1:1-11; Psalm 110; Ephesians 1:15-23; Luke 24:44-53

✝ In the Name of the Father and of the Son and of the Holy Spirit. Amen.

A small group of Anglicans gathers tonight to celebrate in word, song and sacrament the ascended Jesus Christ. Some might see this as a gathering of nostalgics, looking to the past for orientation, huddling around an old-fashioned ritual for some comfort, gathered at some remove from a world that's moved on. Little do they know! The Ascension of Jesus looks forward, not backward – forward to the coming fulfilment of all things in Jesus Christ, of which the Ascension is a sign and a foretaste. And rather than looking inward tonight, away from the challenges of life in the real world, the Ascension drives us outward in hopeful engagement with the real world – the world that tonight, in faith and imagination, we see as coming under the Lordship of the Risen Jesus Christ. The faith of Ascension Day is a faith that gives confidence and clarity of purpose to the Church – to know our mission, to find our voice, to live and speak our good news.

Our readings tonight offer meditations setting out this vision, a vision of confident Christian faith in its fullness, and of our lives in light of that faith. In our Gospel, Luke imagines the moment when the disciples made their big breakthrough, when at last they understood the meaning of Jesus' perplexing suffering and death, his resurrection, and the mission he was giving them – that is, to be clothed with Jesus' own power, right in the city where they lived, and thus to become proclaimers of repentance and forgiveness of sins in Jesus' name to all the nations.

This passage comes at the end of the Gospel; it's the final act when all is revealed, when at last Jesus is fully appreciated, when at last Jesus is worshipped in his own right. And the way Luke imagines this breakthrough in understanding for the disciples is with this story of Jesus exalted to God's place, to God's status – exalted as fulfiller of the Scriptures, which he was able to interpret; exalted as key to the meaning of life, and of God, and of history.

So, to believe this about Jesus, to look to him and to his story for your bearings in life, is the main content of belief in the Ascension. The faith of Ascension Day is faith in Jesus' life and death and ongoing life with us as uniquely real, as uniquely reliable, as uniquely significant; and it's also faith in our own unique role as his witnesses, as his messengers, as his ambassadors, as his *sacraments* even, you and me. This is what Ascension means. It's not primarily, or even necessarily, an eyewitness account of Jesus going up into the sky; rather, it's a poetic rendering of Jesus' attractiveness, of his Lordship, of his energising offer of meaning and purpose for the whole of our lives.

Luke gives us a different version of how the Ascension went at the start of his second volume, the Acts of the Apostles, from which we also hear tonight. There, he gives us forty days to think it over, to get used to the idea. Perhaps this reflects the fact that it took a while for the early Christians to really understand Jesus and what he meant for them, just as it's taken you and me years to grow to our present stage of faith and understanding. Indeed, we know from church history that it took Christians centuries to sort out good, better and best in their thinking about Jesus, about his divinity and humanity, in the age of the Church's creeds. Luke's forty days in the Acts reading today reminds us of what our personal and our collective experience teaches: that coming properly to understand these things takes time.

But when the early Christians do come to understand, according to today's Acts reading, they're imagined as experiencing Jesus' Ascension. And immediately a story about their explosion onto the world stage begins, a story full of their adventures, of their triumphs, of their failings, of their world-shaking faith. But isn't it interesting – and here's my point – isn't it interesting that a book about the doings of apostles, and their Church, begins with this story about God's action, about God vindicating Jesus, and giving his power to Christians to change the world, so that thereafter any story about what the Church is doing, any story about what we're doing as Christians, is first of all a story of what God's doing? In other words, the story of our Christian life and our mission is first and foremost God's story. This is Ascension Day faith, according to our Acts reading today. And it's a cure for any who despair of the Church as an institution. The Church is God's business, and God will not abandon it.

So, let me sum up my understanding of Ascension Day faith. It's not another addition to a long list of things we have to believe about Jesus, things – I might add – that many people find unlikely, like this image of him going up into the air. No, instead of another thing we have to believe about Jesus, *Ascension Day faith is a comprehensive statement of the one key thing that we're invited to believe about Jesus*: that Jesus is Lord, and that our lives are part of his life, part of his mission.

To believe this is to find a new courage and a new resolve to boldly be the Church at a time when that's not always an easy thing. To believe this is properly to understand the poetic image of Jesus ascending through the heavens to God's right hand. To believe this, as the great Collect for Ascension Day puts it, means that we too can "also in heart and mind there ascend, and with him continually dwell, who lives and reigns with you and the Holy Spirit, one God, in glory everlasting. Amen".

Putting the Powers on Notice

Sunday after Ascension / Last Sunday of Easter, Year C, 2 June 2019,
St Philip's, O'Connor.

Acts 16:16-34; Psalm 97; Revelation 22:12-22; John 17:20-26

† In the Name of the Father and of the Son and of the Holy Spirit. Amen.

Friends, this week our Easter Season draws to a close. The Sunday after Ascension, the last Sunday of Easter, is the one before Pentecost, then comes Trinity, then the long run of green Sundays after Pentecost right through to Christ the King in November – which we used to call Ordinary Sundays, until we realised that this sounded a bit too underwhelming. And over these current Sundays marking the transition, we pack in a lot of spiritual insight and a lot of vocational self-discovery for God's people.

At Easter, Jesus dies the death of the scapegoat victim, liquidated for the sake of keeping the peace in that violent way that's still so popular. But then, in the Resurrection, God turns the tables on all that and sets the cat among the pigeons ever after – the world needn't be like that anymore; let's try something different.

One dimension of God's glory revealed in Jesus' resurrection – a non-violent, lump-in-the-throat-type of glory, a world transforming type of glory – is the story of Jesus' Ascension, which the Church marked last Thursday. It's not a story about Jesus achieving escape velocity or anything fundamentalist like that. Rather, it's a way of transitioning from Jesus' visible presence to the new mode of his presence through the Holy Spirit, poured out in the upper room of the last Supper according to John, and on the Old Testament Feast of Pentecost according to Luke. Through Easter to Pentecost, as the shape of this new reality emerges in the early Christian imagination, Jesus is recognised for who he most truly is. In Christian hearts and minds, he's now recognised as sharing in his Father's glory, sitting at the right hand of God – as God's right hand man if you like – set above every power and threat in the world, lifting up our hearts, and putting our fatalism on notice.

Then at Pentecost the nature of Jesus' presence with us is celebrated – present in his Spirit sent from God to shape Jesus' mind and to establish Jesus' life here in the Holy Church. The early Christians were convinced that Jesus continued his mission of bringing God among us in the here and now. He wasn't a dead founder to whom we look back with thanks, but a living saviour who's with us still – who's welcomed in the Eucharistic community with joy, and with the fruit of changed lives. And finally, on Trinity Sunday, Christians testify that we've had to continue the Old Testament's rethinking of God because of Jesus, who was dead but is now alive in the Spirit among us. So, whatever "God" might once have meant, we have this run of Sundays at the end of the Easter season to remind us of who God has become for Christians. Today's Sunday after Ascension is an important stage on the way. So, what do we learn about God today, and what do we learn about ourselves as Christians?

The key thing is that there's been a changing of the guard. The risen, ascended Jesus is now revealed as Lord of the universe. The Game of Thrones is coming to an end, and the violent, pagan pretenders who repress humanity are put firmly on notice. In our psalm today, the storms, the mountains, the heavens – the realms where pagan divinities held sway – are now declared to be the property of our God, the God of Israel's covenant, so that God's righteous and faithful people can rejoice: "Free at last, free at last, Lord God almighty, we're free at last ...".

An example of that freedom, that putting-on-notice of the powers, is there in our Acts reading this morning, with Paul and Silas locked up in the pagan town of Philippi for messing with the status quo. And here the Holy Spirit stages a jailbreak. The message for us is that God's word, God's mission, and our part in it – if we're up for it – is unstoppable. In the face of this, the Roman Empire is at a complete loss, represented by that hapless jailer. And in the conversion and baptism of his family by Paul and Silas, we see the Church's power, its mission *and its future* revealed for all to see.

In our Revelations reading today, we're right at the end of the Bible, and we're invited to claim our place in the heavenly city, having let go of the pagan ways that used to make our world go around, with all the lying and murdering. If that's what we want, according to today's reading, then all we'll get is plague and exclusion, which constitute the actual law of history if you think about it. But here for us instead the Spirit and the bride extend their invitation to the heavenly city: today the Holy Spirit in the Holy Church summons us *here* to be with Christ *there*, now and forever. And isn't this ultimately a Eucharistic invitation, to the thirsty who cherish this water of life Sunday by Sunday?

Then, friends, in our Gospel reading today the connections are all made for us. No wonder people call this fourth gospel a mystical gospel. But it's not for remote adepts or cave-dwelling gurus. It's for the likes of you and me: to be caught up in the glory of God, to realise that in the risen, ascended Jesus the fullness of God is summoning and welcoming us, making us into a Church that can reveal that life-giving glory and hand it on. And we do it through our mutual love in the Church, through our unity. That way we prove that our eyes and our hearts have been lifted up to something far greater than the petty squabbles and immature games-playing that human beings typically prefer, and not least in the Church.

Friends, we can aim higher than that; we can claim a better address than that, and here in the Eucharist we can find that glory, along with our part in it. More of this next Sunday and the one after that, with Pentecost and Trinity. In the meantime, for us today, there's that invitation from the end of the Bible that makes us what we are as Christians:

Ascension

The Spirit and the bride say,
  "Come."
And let everyone who hears say,
  "Come."
And let everyone who is thirsty
  come.
Let anyone who wishes to take
  the water of life as a gift (Revelation 22:17).

The Lord be with you ...

Caught in the Updraft

Sunday after Ascension / Last Sunday of Easter, Year B,
16 May 2021, St Philip's,

Acts 1:15-17, 21-26; Psalm 1; 1 John 5:9-13; John 17:6-19

☦ In the Name of the Father and of the Son and of the Holy Spirit. Amen.

Sometime or other, you may have been questioned about your Christian belief or wondered about it yourself – about belief in God, perhaps, or about belief in Jesus Christ, which is woven inextricably into Christian belief in God as our readings testify today. Many Christians don't make that strong connection themselves, content with Jesus the moral teacher and God as a remote hypothesis. Or, if their God is more personal, their belief may not be at all specific. And many Christians describe their belief as a very private thing, which brings further difficulties when they're confronted by that line in the creed about believing in the Church, which can seem pretty dubious, derivative, and perhaps just an optional extra to Christian believing.

Yet today's readings also weave the Church inextricably into Christian belief in God and in Christ: "As you have sent me into the world", says John's Jesus to his Father in our Gospel, "so I have sent them into the world". This is what abiding in the vine means and being chosen by Jesus rather than our choosing him – the message of Christian belonging that Fr Martin explained last week, and which needs to be explained since many Christians can't make much sense of it.

Today, on this last Sunday of the Easter Season, the Sunday after Ascension, we're invited to consider the questions and perplexities of Christian belief from another perspective. Not as speculative outsiders with minds already formed by other agendas and priorities, who then ask how God and Christ – let alone Church – might fit in with those agendas and priorities. This is how the question of belief is often asked and, sadly, even answered today. Rather, today's readings remind us that we come at believing in God and Christ and Church as insiders, not outsiders.

The leading Australian Catholic theologian, Fr Tony Kelly, has a lovely image of the Church caught in the updraft of the Ascension.[6] I'm going to expand on that. Imagine looking out on a clear Summer's day over an expanse of countryside when the gliding club is busy getting itself aloft. You watch glider after glider circling and climbing in an updraft, like eagles do. They find that cylinder of rising hot air and up they go, lofted together without the need for individual engines – caught up collectively, graciously, with the necessary effort limited to sticking together and not losing the updraft.

Friends, this is how to understand today's readings, so that our believing and doubting are put into a properly Christian context. Our Christian believing is formed within the community of those who've learned to think about God through Jesus Christ, to know Jesus Christ as God with us, which takes place within the nurturing environment of Christian togetherness, of word and sacrament. Christian faith begins within the Church's fellowship rather than isolated in the secular imagination where belief in God and Christ and Church are separated and typically regarded as optional.

When John's Jesus warns his disciples in today's Gospel that the world will reject them just as it rejected him, because they don't belong to the world, this reflects the Church's odd position as I've been presenting it. We stand apart from a world of competing beliefs, stubbornly held positions, fake news, and violent ideologies,

---

6 See Anthony J. Kelly, *Upward: Faith, Church, and the Ascension of Christ* (Collegeville, MN.: Liturgical Press [Michael Glazier], 2014)

because we receive faith in Jesus Christ as a gift that lifts us into a different world, and takes us there together, not leaving us as isolated seekers or else as competing rivals.

So, if Jesus is Lord, which is the message of Ascension, then his Lordship means liberation from the culture wars, from cancel culture, from Trump's Big Lie, from selling out to cynical self-interest, and from religion used as a harsh weapon of social control. In other words, orthodox Christian credal belief in the nexus of God, Christ and Church represents a freeing participation rather than an assertion of superiority over anyone, or else a half-belief that we can't really justify against all the other things in this secular world that we take more seriously.

So, let's not stumble into trying to argue or justify Christian belief on the same ground that unbelievers and disbelievers occupy – not in our pastoral ministry, not in our parenting or grandparenting, and not in our own dark moments of doubt or confusion. Instead, let's remember that we don't approach Christian believing as isolated spectators on the ground, but as participants caught up together in the updraft of Jesus' Ascension, where we're blessed with a different perspective. And the proof of this doctrinal pudding is in the eating, which comes through our giving ourselves together to the life of faith, standing together in the Eucharist and lifting up our hearts as God and the priest invite us to do.

One last thing in this discussion of what Catholic belief is and how Catholic believing works. Pentecost and Trinity Sunday are just around the corner, when this picture of Christian life in God is made complete: at Pentecost, the Catholic Church, all of it in one room, is drawn into God's own life in Christ through the Holy Spirit, and this Trinitarian language shapes how God is to be known and celebrated ever after. But in Luke's telling of the story, which we're following in the book of Acts, the Holy Spirit does something today in the gap that Luke gives us between Jesus' Ascension and the pouring out of his Spirit on the whole Church at Pentecost. Today we hear about the symbolic number twelve being restored to the apostolic band, after the death of Judas the betrayer. The Spirit helps them choose Matthias and so the Church's link to the twelve tribes of Israel, connecting God's past and future faithfulness, is re-established. What I notice here is that the Spirit is not poured out on the whole Church until the Church has been prepared to receive it – until the Spirit has given the Church a structure suitable for receiving and nurturing this gift.

The calling of apostles back then, and of their successors the bishops ever since, represents the next instalments of the Spirit's gift at Pentecost. This is a piece of Catholic wisdom about how God works, and it's a different story than the one you'll hear from Christians who claim individual authority from the Spirit, and especially when the Spirit supposedly tells them to reject and separate themselves from other Christians. This is not to downplay the role of the Spirit in guiding the Church from the bottom up in favour of a clericalism that looks for God's guidance and authority from the top down. It's simply the recognition that God leads the Church both structurally as well as charismatically, with a place for episcopal order as well as general inspiration. And church history, to my reading of it, is a story of both principles working together.

Friends, this is all part of being caught up together in the updraft, rather than puttering around in the atmosphere under our own steam, making what we can of God and Christ, let alone the Church. The God who evokes and invites our believing gives us more help than that.

The Lord be with you ...

Pentecost

Witness, Weaver and Warrior

Pentecost, 19 May 2002, Year A,
St Paul's, Manuka

Acts 2:1-21; Psalm 104:26-36; 1 Corinthians 12:1-13; John 20:19-23

† In the Name of the Father and of the Son and of the Holy Spirit. Amen.

We live in a new romantic era – an era in which whims are sacred, and feelings are paramount, an era when the intensity of experience beats the meaning of experience hands down. As the first romantic era was a protest against dry, scientific rationality in the European Enlightenment, so our own romantic era is suspicious of too much order, too much reason, too much conviction, too much structure. Freedom, expressiveness, disinhibition – these are today's seldom-questioned ideals, at the expense of responsibility, restraint and reliability.

And the notion of spirit is implicated. "Spirit" and "spirituality" are back big-time in our age of relativism, market-driven values and deregulated lifestyle choices. Designer spirituality is the thing. The spirit has become the libidinous energy of our fast-paced culture; the spirit means variety, escape, intoxication, peak-experience, doesn't it? It's youth, it's exuberance, it's "the vibe".

Is this what we're here to celebrate in Church today, this deregulated, non-specific, will-o-the-wisp spirit? Are these red balloons in Church today full of happy gas? Or do we celebrate something more substantial? Do we rejoice today, on this festival day of the Holy Spirit, in something with fibre, something with muscle; do we rejoice in something with warmth and life aplenty, but not flighty, not errant, not effervescent? I think that we do. I think that the Holy Spirit of God presents a substantial alternative to spirituality as it currently reigns in the kingdom of the superficial, of the relativistic. I want to talk to you today not about Holy Spirit as will-o-the-wisp, but Holy Spirit as *witness*, as *weaver*, and as *warrior* – three substantial images doing justice to a substantial spiritual reality.

First, the Holy Spirit of God as *witness*. Witness to what? Witness to Jesus Christ. The Holy Spirit is portrayed in our readings from Scripture today as having a clear, driving vocation, and that is to point us to Jesus, to declare the mighty acts of God in Jesus, and to graft us into what God the Father is doing through Jesus, whom we know as God *with us*, God *for us*. In 1 Corinthians today, Paul tells us that the Holy Spirit brings us to faith in Jesus: "no one can say 'Jesus is Lord' except by the Holy Spirit", Paul writes. Luke gives us his imaginative version of how the Spirit came with tongues of fire in our Acts reading today but it wasn't just pyrotechnics, it was proclamation: "in our own languages we hear them speaking about God's deeds of power". This is the Spirit's work, this is the Church's work, as witness to what God is like, to what God is doing, for which, of course, we look to Jesus.

And we don't just look, we ourselves get caught up in it. This is what John's version of the giving of the Spirit shows us in our Gospel reading today: the Church caught up in Jesus' own ministry, as he breathes his Spirit on his disciples gathered in the upper room, in the room of the last supper. He breathes it on the Church gathered for the Eucharist, I venture to suggest: "he breathed on them and said to them, 'Receive the Holy Spirit. If you forgive the sins of any, they are forgiven them; if you retain the sins of any, they are retained'". In other words, the Holy Spirit catches the Church up into Jesus' own ministry of discernment, and into his confrontation with evil in all its forms.

Jesus through the Holy Spirit empowers the Church to identify, to name, to confront and to overcome evil, and it's for this reason that the authority to absolve sinners is given to every Anglican priest at ordination – an authority from Christ, exercised in and on behalf of the Church, to be liberating agents in a world where evil so often sucks the life out of people. Thus, the Spirit as witness brings us into the orbit of Christ and his mission, making us witnesses, making us Christ for the world. As you can see, this is no will-o-the-wisp Spirit. This is a Spirit with a face, a name and a purpose.

The second image of Holy Spirit I offer you today is Spirit as *weaver*. This is an image of creation, of gathering together, of making something new out of varied elements. The spirit imagined in an age like ours, an age of relativism and indifference to truth, is a spirit that fragments, that isolates people in the intensity but ultimately the meaninglessness of experience. But the Holy Spirit of God is a weaver, a patternmaker, a force of creation and re-creation. Our Psalm today sees the Spirit of God at the heart of creation, giving us a universe not a pluriverse: "When you send forth your Spirit they are created, and you renew the face of the earth".

And not only the physical world, but a new world for human beings is the Spirit's work. There's a lot of interest in multiculturalism nowadays, and the political cake is cut according to whether unity or diversity is top priority in your thinking about society. (More of this next week, on Trinity Sunday, the great festival of unity in diversity.) But for now, note how the Holy Spirit in our readings today weaves a unity out of strikingly diverse elements. In Acts, the list of cultures and places named is a sign of this diversity, thoroughly polyglot: "Parthians. Medes. Elamites" through to "Cretans and Arabs" – enormously diverse, yet united in hearing the mighty acts of God. The tower of Babel from Genesis, and the perennial curse of miscommunication and tribalism and opposition that came with it, is symbolically reversed at Pentecost; a powerful Spirit from God weaves the diversity of our human race into a new creation.

This new creation is sacramentally present in the Church, thanks to God's Spirit, according to Paul today. A diverse community of diverse gifts and diverse identities is woven by God's

Spirit. So radical is this unity of purpose and action that Paul uses images of the human body, in which many parts perfectly cohere: "For in the one Spirit we were all baptised into one body – Jews or Greeks, slaves or free – and we were all made to drink of one Spirit". This mix of people in the Church crosses every social and racial boundary, and every visceral urge to exclude is confronted by it. The Spirit poured out even on slaves, according to the Acts reading, introduces a shocking challenge to every sensitivity about pedigree in the Church. It challenges everyone who would divide a congregation into "A list" and "B list"; it confronts natural human flocking together with birds of a feather.

Instead, we have God's own shocking, tasteless, unaccountable love for all of us, be we suave or gauche, be we witty or plodding, be we accomplished or awkward, be we "the right sort of people" or "not the right sort of people". And thank God for this weaving work of the Holy Spirit, to which the Church can give witness in its own life – thank God we're not left with the bitter tribalism and the endless mutual hatred and suspicion that's the stuff of human history. To move beyond this is God's gift to the Church in the Holy Spirit. To resist this weaving Spirit and insist on clubbiness and tribalism in the Church is to betray the work of God's Spirit. A cliquey Church is a blasphemy, pure and simple.

A final image of the Spirit I want to offer today is Holy Spirit as *warrior*. This is a masculine image to match the feminine image of weaver. The coming of God's Spirit is confronting and offensive. "They are filled with new wine" is the derisive putdown; they're the sort of disreputable people who drink cheap wine in public. The coming of God's Spirit is guaranteed to upset people, because by breaking down boundaries it abolishes advantage, it gives people ideas, it sets a violent force abroad for change and renewal, and of course this sort of thing always comes up against vested interests. The imagery of the Acts reading today is apocalyptic: "I will show portents in the heaven above and signs in the earth below. The sun shall be turned to darkness and the moon to blood". In other words, the coming of the Spirit means that all bets are off, that the world is judged, that the real things of God are revealed. As Yeats put it,

> The blood-dimmed tide is loosed, and everywhere
> The ceremony of innocence is drowned.[7]

The Spirit as a warrior is an image of the world challenged and its evils overcome.

Remember too the share we have through the Spirit in Jesus' ministry: "whose sins you forgive they are forgiven, who's sins you retain they are retained". This is the warrior dimension of the Christian life: not sentimental, not pious, not nice and non-judgmental. No, it's a more violent and decisive business altogether, to be caught up in God's Spirit. It makes us discerning, wise, able to see through nonsense and make up our minds. This is the energy of the warrior, this single-mindedness. And it's the Spirit's gift in this place here this morning, as the deep truth and purpose of things is laid bare for us in word and sacrament. So, instead of romantic, dissolute, unfocused and dilettantish, the stuff of God's Spirit at Pentecost has content. The Holy Spirit of God is about witness to Jesus Christ, it weaves a new creation and sets that new creation as a sign to the world in the form of the Church; and it unleashes a warrior energy to galvanise us in a culture that's irresolute and indifferent. The Holy Spirit of God as witness, weaver, and warrior is a wake-up call for our culture, and on this feast of Pentecost we the Church are summoned once again to live as if we believed it.

The Lord be with you...

---

7   W. B. Yeats, "The Second Coming", online at https://www.poetryfoundation. org/poems/43290/the-second-coming (last accessed August 2022).

A Blow-up Church?

Pentecost, Sunday 15 May 2005, Year A,
St Paul's, Manuka

Numbers 11:24-30; Psalm 104:26-36; Acts 2:1-21; John 20:19-23

✝ In the Name of the Father and of the Son and of the Holy Spirit. Amen.

What do you do if you can't decide between a church wedding and a garden wedding? Well, one enterprising Englishman has come up with an inflatable church that you can pump-up in your favourite outdoor location, thus solving the problem. That's right, you lay it out on the ground like a life raft and attach the air hose, and before you know it, the reassuring shape lurches upright, complete with arches, buttresses and even stained-glass windows. You can imagine how popular this blow-up church has proved to be, can't you? It's caused outrage in some dignified Church of England circles, appearing to be the antithesis of what a real church should be, which is all solid, old and reassuringly traditional.

But today on Pentecost Sunday, on this Feast Day of the Holy Spirit and birthday of the Christian Church, I want to suggest that this mad inventor has actually got it right; I want to suggest a truer understanding of the Church – that the Church is more an event in the here and now, inflated by the Holy Spirit, than it is a venerable structure looking for its identity in the past. Here at St Paul's today, we've got the structure, as ever, onto which the festive red Pentecost balloons have been attached. But what if the balloons were the real thing and all the structures of our Church were secondary? What if God's Holy Spirit is the main game in Christian faith, not the add-on?

Now, this is strange talk – it's strange to hear it in a mainstream Church like our Anglican Church, which hasn't been significantly transformed by the Charismatic movement, and it's strange to hear it in the Western Church, which in its creed has the Holy Spirit proceeding not just from the Father – as in the Eastern Orthodox Churches – but from the Son as well, which means that we in the West have refused to de-regulate the Holy Spirit quite like they have in the East, keeping the Holy Spirit linked to the gold-standard of Church traditions and structures that mediate Jesus and his Gospel.

Yet we in the Western Church risk over-investing in structure. Our Roman Catholic cousins have their infallible papacy. It might seem that the rushing wind of the Spirit, by and large, is being confined to the corridors of the Vatican, and to the past pronouncements of Church authority. And our many and various Protestant cousins aren't too different. The conservative ones have an infallible Bible, the literal truth of which reassures them in all perplexities of the present. So, instead of such Protestants having a flesh and blood Pope, they find in their Bible what's been called "a paper pope". And, just like the Roman Catholics, their problem is how to ensure that the truth and power of what happened back then is preserved and protected so it gets through to us intact today. The gap between us and the formative events of our faith is large, and frightening, according to this view, and we worry about adequate mediation across the chasm of history.

And if you're not a conservative but a liberal in theology, the same problem reappears in subtly different form. Perhaps you come to doubt the historical truthfulness of much that's in the Bible, with nothing left for your faith to rest on. The phenomenal success of Dan Brown's ecclesiastical bodice-ripper *The Da Vinci Code* is proof positive that for many in the West today, the historical evidence for Christian origins has been fatally compromised – who was Jesus *really*, was he what the Gospels say he was, and can the Church be trusted not to conceal the unpalatable truth for its own ends? Many of today's Westerners need little encouragement to abandon the Church and its claims for Jesus in the light of challenges like these. And how does the liberal Christian respond? By reasserting enough historical reliability by scholarly means, so that the broad truth of the Gospel portrait of Jesus can be affirmed as reliable, even if a lot of allegory and storytelling in the New Testament is admitted. Thus, we turn not to the pope and his infallible teaching office, and not to an infallible Bible, but to a *papacy of professors*, as it's been called, to ensure that our link to secure Christian origins is maintained.

And what about normal Anglicans? Very often in our Church these days the problem is one of nostalgia for traditions, and a preference for the past. Give me the old service, give me the old hymns, give me the old certainties. Even relatively recent tradition is better than current innovation: give me the old Rector! At its best, this Anglican love of the past is a stable anchor against senseless innovation, and more likely attuned to the wellsprings of faith, so that it deserves respect. But at its worst it's a counsel of despair, so that Australian Anglicanism is full of the walking wounded, whose link with the things of God through the Church is tenuous, with a resultant widespread mood in our Church of weary, nostalgic defeatism.

Can you see that in all these cases, Catholic and Protestant, conservative and liberal, mainstream Anglican as well, the crisis is one of felt separation from the wellsprings of faith, and the need to find a secure way through to the bedrock of Christian origins, one way or another.

Oh, and one further option. If we're still of a mind to preserve our Christian faith, but we can't reliably connect to our origins anymore – if we can't really make sense of our doctrines and trust the structures and traditions and hierarchies of our Church anymore – then we can replace them with something else. Thus, the serious, *helpful* Church we so often try to be these days: the community group *helping* a lonely populace to find connection, or else an agency of social work, reliably stoking political enthusiasms of the left. We become a Church desperately seeking *relevance* now that faith and conviction have worn thin. Hence the rise of managerialism, glossy spiral-bound programs for mission and evangelism, strategic planning, and the bishop reinvented as CEO in our Church.

This is a culture I laboured under in Adelaide in my last appointment, and one with which I took strong issue in the last chapter of my recent book on the church,[8] but which I fear is the way of the future for the broad middle of Australian Anglicanism, at least for the next decade – for the non-ideological part of our Church, that is, neither high nor low, neither Anglo-Catholic nor Evangelical.

So, if nerviness and a sense of disconnection is the problem for all sorts of Churches in the West today, ours included – of being cut adrift from a reliable past, of a declining confidence in structure and authority – then for God's sake what can we do? I'm suggesting today that God has done what needs doing already, and that Pentecost is the clue. Pentecost reminds us that God does not leave us disconnected, disempowered and flailing about to keep our heads above water in a situation of Godlessness, powerlessness and hopelessness.

Now, of course, structure is important, and our Psalm celebrates it today – all the wonderful order of the natural world. But the Spirit of God is necessary to animate that structure, or it will fail, and things will die and return to their dust. Structure is important, and the prophetic office of religious leadership given to Moses is a sure foundation of God's provision for Israel. But in our Numbers reading today, the Lord begins to put the Spirit onto others among God's people, reaching beyond the traditional structures, and old father Moses has enough wit to welcome the new thing.

---

8   Scott Cowdell, *God's Next Big Thing: Discovering the Future Church* (Melbourne: John Garratt, 2004).

Indeed, the pouring out of God's Spirit on the infant Church at Pentecost, with tongues of fire and other signs of the final apocalypse breaking into the present, is a sign that God in a new event is reconstituting the faith and life of God's people. Beyond the world as we know it – divided, everyone talking at cross purposes, all violence and exclusion – God is establishing a new community of mutual understanding, of mutual good will, around the good news of Jesus Christ.

This new world that God is creating by God's Holy Spirit comes home to roost with a fresh understanding of the Church in our Gospel reading today. Jesus risen calls the Church together in peace – "Peace be with you"; the same words we'll say to each other in a few moments' time – and in the face of all the world's divisions, all the world's antipathies, all the world's violence, Jesus shows the marks of that violence to us in his own pierced hands and side and he says "with you, the world begins again". And so, we come to share his discernment, we come to freedom and we bring others to freedom by the power of his judgment, active among us: "whose sins you forgive they are forgiven, whose sins you retain they are retained".

Thus, we become the people who know and name the deep truth of God. This truth is not remote from us in a past we have to protect, but alive among us in a present we can't deny and in a future that beckons us forward, beyond all the seemingly intractable divisions and self-destructiveness of human history. Hence, our greeting of peace in the Eucharist is a sign of a new world being born in the Spirit of God – not a secret club handshake, and not just the goodwill of mutual regard, but the discipline of mutual openness, whether we like each other or not.

And so I come to the point I'm wanting to make today about the Holy Spirit of God in the Church. The Holy Spirit establishes the Church as a living, present reality of God – yes, it happened back then; yes, our beliefs about Jesus and our structures of Church authority, our venerable traditions, are all mediators of that reality.

But without the Holy Spirit of God turning past truth into present conviction, turning venerable structure into contemporary event, then it's not the Church of God. Without the Spirit, with Christ only – with his Gospel, with his sacraments, with his ministers, but without the Spirit – God has one hand tied behind God's back. St Irenaeus called the Word and the Spirit the two hands of God, and it's a good image. God works through Word, through Gospel, through structure, through tradition, reaching back to Christ. But God also works through Spirit, the Holy Spirit who raised Jesus from the dead, who was poured out to found the Church, and who brings the Church alive today in every place, in every heart, turning a structure into an event.

At their best, the Eastern Orthodox theologians are right onto this, and one of the best of them, John Zizioulas, puts it very simply: "Christ *in-stitutes*, and the Spirit *con-stitutes*".[9] In other words, God's Holy Spirit constitutes the Church, constitutes its faith as a living reality that incorporates *us*, you and me, making faith a real, personal event, and making Christ a living, present reality for us – not the remote founder of an institution that mediates him from a great distance, and to which many Western Christians cling by the skin of their teeth.

Nothing I'm saying today should be read as critique of Gospel, of creed, of institution, of Church authority. But without the Holy Spirit of God *constituting* everything that God *instituted* in Christ, there might be the sausage, but there's no sizzle!

In closing, I reiterate my point that the Church is not just a creation of the Word, an institution that looks to the past for its origins, but instead it's an event of God's Spirit constituted as a fresh start every time – indeed, in every Eucharist, where at the *epiclesis*, the calling down of the Holy Spirit, the priest calls on God to renew the Church in the Holy Spirit, to unite it in the body of God's son,

---

9   John Zizioulas, *Being as Communion: Studies in Personhood and the Church* (Crestwood, NY.: St Vladimir's Seminary Press, 1997), 140.

and bring it to the future perfection of which every Eucharist is an anticipation.

So, friends, the Spirit makes the Church. The best model of the Church is not the gothic mausoleum, then, a structure into which we struggle to breathe life, but a Church inflated by the Spirit rather than deflated by the long haul of history. And it's a lot more fun, too – a blow-up church, like an inflatable castle, with you and me and all the creatures of God's new creation bouncing round inside it. The Church is anything but a structure that must be desperately preserved, fretted over, propped up by some whiz-bang strategy, or else morosely abandoned.

The Lord be with you...

Beyond Cynicism,
Fatalism and Groupthink

Pentecost, 20 May 2018, Year B,
St Philip's, O'Connor

Acts 2:1-21; Psalm 104:26-36; Romans 8:22-27;
John 15:26-27; 16:4b-15

† In the Name of the Father and of the Son and of the Holy Spirit. Amen.

I know that many of you were glued to the screen last night watching Prince Harry and Meghan Markle getting married. Annabel Crabb, on the ABC News website, said that it's a funny wedding when the bride gets upstaged by the clergy. But that's what happened. The Presiding Bishop of the Episcopal Church of the United States stunned a lukewarm, nominally Church of England, upper-class congregation with a dose of lively African American preaching. They'd never seen anything like it! Now, I don't know if I can match Bishop Michael Curry's delivery, but the material before us on this Pentecost Sunday makes me want to try. What I want to do today, as we celebrate the sending of God's Holy Spirit and the calling of God's Holy Church, is to contrast the spirit of this world, as the Bible calls it, with the Holy Spirit of God.

The spirit of this world creates an in-group, a dynasty, a clique, a faction, a tribe, a community, a nation, a civilisation, a religion, by excluding and demonising something and someone else. It doesn't matter if you're a tribal Catholic or a devout atheist, a smug Anglican or a Pentecostal zealot; it doesn't matter if you're on the radical green Left or the coal-fired Right. All that matters to the spirit of this world is that we know who the sinners are, that we know who the righteous are, and we know who deserves judgment, so that everything comes out in our favour. We all know people and places and movements like this; the spirit of this world represents a constant human temptation that we all fall into.

And, friends, the tragic irony is that whenever we claim the spiritual high ground, presuming to attack and root out the spirit of this world when we see it at work in others, we end up falling into it ourselves. The spirit of this world is a mimetic vortex from which we can't escape by our own strength. It shapes our language, our sense of race, gender and class, of being able or disabled, of being a success or a failure. Our only escape from the spirit of this world, our only way to recognise it and break free of it, is to sign up instead to the Holy Spirit of God. And, friends, all this is set out in today's Gospel.

There we recognise God's Holy Spirit as our advocate for the defence, as René Girard puts it. Jesus tells his disciples in today's Gospel that the Holy Spirit comes to declare the world wrong about sin, about righteousness and about judgment.

Why is the world wrong about sin? It's wrong about sin because, as Jesus goes to the cross, God lines up alongside the sinners, alongside the offscourings of human contempt. There, on a rubbish dump outside Jerusalem, cursed and condemned by both the religious nationalists and the pagan occupiers, who find themselves in sickening but predictable accord, Jesus reveals the mechanism that makes our world go round – the spirit of this world, that is – and he puts a spanner in the works. God's Holy Spirit, the advocate for the defence, stands up for the condemned and despised in Jesus' name, pointing to the one who now occupies the place of greatest honour at God's right hand, when all the world could manage was to despise and crucify him.

Next, why is the world wrong about righteousness? Because no-one can boast that they're in the right, no-one can stand swathed in their own rectitude while pointing an accusing finger at others, when Jesus Christ himself seeks out that very place of universal condemnation. So, friends, whenever righteousness eludes us, and whatever moral accomplishment we might lack, the shameful place of unrighteousness is where our God chooses to be, close to the failed and the broken, revealed today as their advocate for the defence.

And why is the world wrong about judgment? Because that other, malign spirit, the spirit of this world, is the spirit that's litigious, prosecuting, and judgmental, eager to even the score. And because human beings and human groups are typically like this, we tend to imagine God like this in our own image – we tend to think of God's judgment as the kind of vengeful payback that we know all too well.

Yet today in our Gospel, God the Holy Spirit, who points to the revealing, saving work of God the Son, stands not against us but *for* us, as advocate for the defence. Yes, God the Father does judge, but what's judged and condemned is the spirit of this world, the spirit that connives and excludes, that damns and lynches. And what does God's judgment look like? It looks like vindication! God judges a humanity in love with death and with having the last word by raising Jesus from the dead, pouring out the Holy Spirit, igniting a countermovement in human history called the Church.

God's judgment doesn't let us get away with making history all about cynicism, fatalism and groupthink. Instead, God's judgment liberates us from our worst selves by breaking the power of evil, which is a traditional way of putting all this, enlisting us in a pattern of personal and ecclesial life beyond anything that we're capable of on our own – which we call eternal life.

Now, friends, this good news becomes the charter of a whole new worldview, a new religion, a new set of spiritual practices. Let me make three points about this, from our other readings this morning. First, from our Acts reading, we have that marvellous multicultural scene in which Pentecost, the Old Testament festival of the law, now marks a new law that grasps the hearts and minds of God's people. No more tower of Babel, which was a story about human division and enmity. Instead, a new humanity is summoned beyond both isolation and totalitarianism. Here the Church emerges not as a social contract between individuals, as some Protestants think, nor as an impersonal collective, as some Roman Catholics think. Rather, the Church is born as a creation of the Holy Spirit in which unity is achieved at no-one's expense, and where everyone is heard and appreciated in their own voice, in their own right. Here is a template for Christian life together. Here the newborn Church stands around Peter its apostolic leader in witness to Jesus – which for Henri de Lubac was the Catholic Church in its fulness present in one room.

Second, if this is what God is like, and if this is what Christians are liberated and enlivened to discover and to live out, then it goes to the foundations of our whole view of creation. The stories of creation told by a world that has it all wrong about sin, righteousness and judgment are very different – a world that imagines reality as conflictual and naturally thinks of God as violent. Hence, we have the widespread ancient mythological stories of creation, which started in Babylon and spread around the pagan world – stories in which the high God slays a monster of chaos to create the world. This chaotic element is typically imagined using imagery of water and drowning. But today's Psalm imagines something different, with all of this put on notice. The key to understanding today's Psalm portion is the image of Israel's God that we see again and again in the Old Testament, who is completely unfazed by the watery chaos of ancient imagination. This is God enthroned above the water flood in another Psalm. This is God's Spirit effortlessly moving over the deep to create the world at the start of Genesis. This is God rolling back Noah's flood, whose chaotic waters will never break out again. And this is the Red Sea, turned into God's theatre of liberation for an enslaved Israel.

Today, in our Psalm, we see this imagery once again: there is the wide immeasurable sea, and there is that Leviathan – there is that personified figure of evil and chaos that the ancients feared, whose pagan gods had to wrestle with it and subdue it. But here that Leviathan becomes God's plaything, formed to sport in the deep. In other words, violence is not at the heart of reality; our God isn't involved in any sort of self-defining struggle against evil, and neither should we over-dramatise ourselves in the same way. Instead, in today's Psalm, God is serenely in charge, with Leviathan demythologised, and made light of – the monster is transformed from "Godzilla" into "Flipper". Likewise, God the Holy Spirit is able to create a better world than the spirit of this world can do, with all its adversarial obsessiveness.

Now, finally, we need to acknowledge the potential difficulty of all this, and how shaky our faith in it can be. This is why St Paul in our Epistle today talks about all creation groaning – and we ourselves groaning, we who have the first fruits of the Spirit. Friends, this is the now and the not yet paradox of Christianity: we affirm by faith the real presence of Christ and his new creation, never more than here in the Eucharist, yet if we're honest we must also acknowledge our own spiritual inadequacy and the times when God seems absent.

But in our Epistle today, Paul invites us to reinterpret those familiar sighs and groans that greet our life's hurts and disappointments, that mark our frustration with ourselves and with the dreadful behaviour and painful situations that all of us have to face. We're invited to read all of this as a sign of God's Holy Spirit at work, praying within us in those all-too-familiar sighs that are too deep for words.

Here we're invited to acknowledge a measure of holy restlessness as the mark of an authentic spiritual life – not a restlessness that gives in to anxiety and obsessiveness, but a restlessness that can be transformed through patient mindfulness into a robust and resolute Christian character, up for any worthwhile challenge.

So, on this feast day of God's Holy Spirit, when Holy Church receives its charter to be the non-judgmental vector of God's liberating, enlivening mission in the world, Christians take comfort and take courage: we have an advocate for the defence, who exposes and overcomes the spirit of this world.

The Lord be with you ...

Trinity Sunday

Good News for Western Culture

Trinity Sunday, 26 May 2002, Year A,
St Paul's, Manuka

Exodus 34:1-8, 2 Corinthians 13:11-13, Matthew 28:16-20

✝ In the Name of the Father and of the Son and of the Holy Spirit. Amen.

For theologians of the fourth century, who gave us the creed we say this morning, and increasingly for theologians today, the Doctrine of the Trinity is Christianity's greatest idea about God, and about the world. The Doctrine of the Trinity is a liberating, energising power pack of good news, and good implications – not just in the world of theology, but for real people living real lives in the real world. That's certainly the way I feel about it. But for many Christians, it's a different story. Rather than good news, the Trinity is indifferent news (because it seems unnecessarily complicated, perhaps, or not very relevant to the way we live our lives). Even for clergy, the whole thing is often a bit much, which is why when I taught in a theological college, my colleagues and I were never short of invitations to preach in parishes on Trinity Sunday.

So, let me try once again to present this idea – the idea that our hearts best incline to God, that our minds best honour and appreciate God, if we name God as Father, Son and Holy Spirit. Why is it so?

I suggest that we need to start with the Bible, though I don't believe the Trinity in its fully developed form can be found in the Bible. We have a Father and a Son and a Holy Spirit in the Bible, nowhere more clearly than in today's missionary charter from Matthew's Gospel. But it took 300 years for the Church to draw the implications about God found in passages like this into a clear, Trinitarian shape. Nevertheless, the Trinity does start with the Bible, and with the experience of God's people reflected in the Bible.

Consider our Old Testament reading today from Exodus, with the giving of God's law. What sort of God do we meet in this marvellous story? I suggest that it's a complex God that we meet here. It's a high and a just and a demanding God, a God who overawes and who silences Moses. But it's also a gracious and a forgiving God, "slow to anger, and abounding in steadfast love and faithfulness", a God who draws near to embrace the cause of God's people and who will never let them go. The God we meet in today's Old Testament reading is a great and terrible God, yet at the same time a God *for us*, a God *with us*.

And if this is the God we meet in the story of Exodus, as in Israel's story more generally throughout the Old Testament, then it's certainly the God we meet in the story of Jesus Christ. Jesus is God with us, the Son of God, which means that he's the one who makes God uniquely present. Today's Gospel of the risen Christ is a Gospel declaring that we, the Church, are caught up in a divine movement, caught up in a mission, in a mysticism even, of being called and sent. But this is not a Jesus who lives in our past and in our memory: rather, it's Jesus *with us*, even to the end of the age – with us as the beating heart of Christian life and mission. Thus, we know the God who sends; thus, we know the one who is sent, and thus *we know the presence with us of this one who is sent*, who sends us in turn.

This complex reality of Christian experience was eventually rendered down into doctrine: our sense of God came over time to be articulated in terms of Father, Son and Holy Spirit. According to the Scots theologian James Mackey, the Trinity is our answer to the question, "what sort of God do we meet in the story of Jesus Christ?" It's the same complex God we meet in the Old Testament, the covenant God, the God *for us*, but now known more clearly as the Christlike God, and as the Holy Spirit who mediates Christ's presence to us and through us.

Well, that's the theology. The next question is, so what? What does this have to do with me, with my life in the world? I had a parishioner once who was a refrigerator mechanic; he said to me one Sunday after Church, "you know what your problem is, Scott? – you think like a theologian!" With him in mind, let me try to bring all of this down to earth. I suggest three areas of significant relevance for Trinitarian belief.

The *first* has to do with problems we get into if we emphasise the grandeur and the distance of God, but forget God's nearness, which is a very common thing to do. In other words, emphasising the Father without the Son or the Spirit. The *second* has to do with the problems we get into if we lose the unifying centre of meaning and value that is God the Father, and instead experience the world as incorrigibly plural, without a centre, as a place of many options but nothing definite. And this, of course, is also a very common state of affairs. In other words, emphasising the Spirit without the Son and the Father. The *third* has to do with seeing it all in the past, with God and Christ as a sort of static tableau that we like to look at, from which we take our bearings in life, but which isn't a transforming, present-day reality for us. In other words, having the Father and the Son without the Spirit.

First, the problem of too much monotheism – of God far but not near; of God the Father without Christ or Spirit. Here I'm not talking about the great monotheistic faiths of Judaism and Islam, but of a particular *Christian* tendency in our Western world since the rise of science in the seventeenth century. It's a tendency to see the world, and the human person, as closed, autonomous systems, with God removed to a great distance. Instead of the world as a spiritual place, a place that can only be fully appreciated with reference to God, in time we in the West opted for the closed weave of nature in which God was no longer at home, in which divine action could only be understood as intervention from outside. And this is the way that a lot of people in our society imagine God to this day: as an occasionally intervening something-or-other, difficult to imaginatively connect with, let alone feel drawn to.

Modern scientific Westerners invented a God with so little to commend him it's no wonder that ours is the culture that embraced atheism, because such bad ideas about God lead to atheism. But the God we're rejecting here isn't the God of Jesus Christ, it isn't the God who embraces us in Holy Spirit. If we knew *this* God, if we knew a God near to our world, near to us, a God who gets alongside us, then there wouldn't be so many atheists around today – many of whom are thoughtful, sensitive, even spiritual people.

In the same way, as the Western world came to imagine our humanity in predominantly individual terms, less communal, more fundamentally isolated than before, so God too became a lonely, self-enclosed individual – a God as remote from us as we at our worst are remote from each other.

But if we proclaim the *Trinitarian* God, we offer an alternative to all this. If we proclaim the Trinitarian God, we mount a protest against disrespect for the earth, against the attitude of contempt for nature that's been such a feature of life in modern Western culture. The spoiling of nature, the careless disregard for our fragile planet earth, goes in tandem with a view of God remote from our world. Thus, we spiritually devalue our world.

In the same way, if God is a lonely individual, then so are we likely to be lonely individuals. But if God is Trinitarian, if God is a community of profoundly related persons, then the crying need for community in a psychologically weary Western world will find profound encouragement. Remember how over a million Australians, many Christians among them, used to stay in on Sunday nights a couple of years back to watch *Seachange* on television. There we saw portrayed what people took to be a "real" community, a community as it should be, "not like the one we're from" – a community of people living close to each other and close to nature. This sort of thing pushes buttons for us, which is why *Seachange* was the most popular program on Australian television.

Clearly, though, the Christian fellowship and its Eucharist fails to push these same buttons, even for many who participate regularly. Clearly, the Trinitarian God is not made manifest for us in the kind of worship and genuine Christian community life that might begin to turn the tide of our lonely imaginations. Isolated individuals worshipping the greatest isolated individual of all will not do it for us – I guarantee it! But the Trinitarian drama of our Eucharist, the mystical drawing of all things by the Spirit into Christ's self-offering to the Father, is a vision that *just might* begin to do it for us – *if* we come to see it that way, *if* our fellowship and teaching are equal to the grandeur that our Eucharistic liturgy paints for us.

The *second* point of relevance I want to make concerns the very opposite problem. We live in a time of collapsing absolutes, and endemic change. Social commentators tell us that this is the major cause of stress of which so many people complain. Ours is a culture that's lost its bearings, it's centre. Many younger people today, who have been called the options generation, have learned to live without many of these comfortable assumptions and foundational ideas that older Australians long took for granted. The confidence that we live in *one world*, with a meaning and a purpose, and a right way to live in it, is tied up with belief in *one God*, who stands behind it all, who is the centre, guaranteeing meaning and purpose. People sense this when they send their children to Sunday School or to Church Schools to learn some values. All that these children often learn, however, is that belief in God is just one more option (some sort of vague, unfocused spirituality, perhaps), which can mean whatever they want it to mean.

On the contrary, the Trinitarian vision is quite particular about God. It recognises the complexity and diversity of experience, to be sure, and actually builds that diversity into the very being of God – a God who is known as three distinct persons. Yet the Trinitarian inner tension holds that diversity in unity, with God the Father grounding every manifestation of the Word and the Spirit of God throughout the world – manifestations that I happen to think are quite diverse.

The real-life relevance here has to do with the way that we so often react to the loss of a unifying centre in life. Often, we make our own centre to fill the gap. So, if people lose belief in God, they erect an idol in God's place to give their life meaning and cohesion – even among "the options generation". For some it's money, or popularity, or looks, or health, or success, all of which we see pursued obsessively. But it's not just individuals who do this. For our society as a whole, it can be a grand ideology that's pursued, like communism. Communism was an atheistic philosophy that replaced God. It replaced God with an infallible state, and with a relentless march of history, neither of which left much room for diversity. And since the fall of global communism, we now have the booming phenomenon of global capitalism, growing on the back of new information technology. This is a Westernised global culture offering great rewards for the innovative and the able, but which steamrolls over local cultures, and over less-well-equipped players, like the poor and the unskilled – those who economics commentator Tom Friedman calls "turtles", desperately trying to avoid becoming roadkill on the information superhighway.

We need to find alternatives to such dehumanising trends. And the vision we celebrate on Trinity Sunday points the way by holding the one and the many together, celebrating diversity without sacrificing unity and helping us resist the prevailing cultural tendency: the tendency to rush into the vacuum created by our culture's death of God, to make new gods in our own image. Yet these are not gods that will liberate and humanise; these are gods that will damn us rather than save us. The Trinitarian God, on the other hand, teaches us the right spiritual geometry for profound social transformation.

Trinity Sunday

Now to my *third* and last area of relevance in this reflection on Trinitarian faith. For many people, God and Christ are like those charming tableaux that we see in department store windows at Christmastime: they're reassuring images and ideas – of sacrifice and goodness and moral rightness – from which we can take our bearings in life. This is a kind of faith that is well represented. But the element of living experience is missing. Here I'm reminded of "dem bones, dem bones, dem dry bones" in the prophet Ezekiel's vision, in need of a spirit to enliven them. The Charismatic Movement in our Church has been a corrective to this sort of dry and dutiful faith. Yet still, many Anglicans miss out on a lively, engaging faith that gives power to belief, that turns religious ideals into passionate commitment, and that turns belief into knowledge of the heart. *It's the Spirit of God that turns faith from a tableau into a drama, making a living reality out of a dried arrangement.* This is why we priests are charged at our ordination to pray earnestly for the Holy Spirit. Because without God's own help, the life of faith can become dry and lifeless, even if we have all the right beliefs.

So, there we are. The Trinity is a wonder of imagination and revelation, and more relevant than we might have thought. It's a cure for atheism, for disrespecting the natural world, and for chronic human aloneness. It points to a centre in the midst of diversity, while keeping us from enthroning something destructive at the centre of our world. And the Trinity is a living God – not a tableau, but a drama. This is why Trinity Sunday crowns our Church year, summing up Easter and Ascension and Pentecost, rendering into doctrine all that we've learned about God.

✝ The grace of the Lord Jesus Christ, the love of God and the fellowship of the Holy Spirit, be with you all...

Trinity Starts with Experience

Trinity Sunday, 3 June 2007, Year C,
St Paul's, Manuka

Proverbs 8:1-4, 22-31; Psalm 8; Romans 5:1-5; John 16:12-15

✝ In the Name of the Father and of the Son and of the Holy Spirit. Amen.

When I was first ordained, twenty years ago, my curacy was at Holy Trinity, Fortitude Valley, in Brisbane's inner city. It was a place of boisterous pubs, illegal gaming, prostitution and knife fights – the sort of demimonde found in waterfront areas worldwide. Since the war, "the Valley", as it's known, filled with light industry as Australia rebuilt. More recently, it came to boast a vibrant Chinatown through Asian immigration while other parts have undergone quite some gentrification. Yet the old flavour remained when I worked there, in a year when all eyes in Australia turned to scandals over the so-called Moonlight State and especially to Fortitude Valley, as Queensland's culture of police and political corruption was exposed. Back then, too, you could still meet the "old Valley characters", as my training Rector, Canon Lyall Turley, used to call them, delighting to send his bookish deacon into their alarming haunts to do home communions.

It was to one such haunt that the Rector took me one day, teaching me the funeral business. An elderly brother and sister had lived together all their lives in the same house, long decades past the death of their parents. Neither had ever married. He'd worked in the factory and she'd looked after him, then they enjoyed a long retirement of quiet togetherness, until out of the blue the brother dropped dead from a heart attack. The Rector needed to prepare an address for the funeral, so he asked the sister to tell him about her brother. Her gaze turned inward for a long moment, reflecting back over nearly nine decades of daily devotion and companionship, until finally she piped up with this: "He barracked for 'Valleys' in the Rugby League".

I was surprised, and a little disappointed, I must say. I'd expected a fuller tribute! But in later years, ministering in similar situations as Rector of my first parish, and still today, I've encountered the same sort of thing. Two common phrases recur. From older widows, looking back on decades of marriage, their simple tribute "he was a good provider". And from children grown into middle age, trying to tell me what their late mother had meant to them, came the unadorned phrase, "her family was everything to her". I came to appreciate that these standard bromides point beyond themselves to something far more detailed, to the stories of a lifetime – the old sister remembering her brother's long life lived close to its roots, his identity part of a tapestry of communal life in Fortitude Valley worn increasingly thin by social change: "He barracked for Valleys in the Rugby League". Or the widow recalling decades of undemonstrative constancy: "he was a good provider". And those middle-aged sons and daughters no doubt struggling themselves to be good parents, remembering the mother who was always there: "For her, family was everything". These stock phrases point beyond themselves to rich stories of faithfulness and belonging, vibrant and personal.

And so it is, friends, with our doctrine of the Trinity. "Three persons, One God" or "three persons sharing one substance" are traditional phrases we use, along with a familiar prayer drawn from St Paul called "the grace", which goes "the grace of the Lord Jesus Christ, the love of God and the fellowship of the Holy Spirit, be with us all evermore". These are tried and true forms of words that roll off the tongue. But behind them stands the long story of our God giving content to these formulae, helping us appreciate their meaning.

The revealing of God as Trinity began in our tradition with a God reaching out to a particular people, in the concrete history of their world. We have the Old Testament stories of Abraham the father of faith, of Moses and the Exodus from slavery of a people chosen for no other reason than God's love and mercy toward them, given a promised land and a heritage, of God's continuing faithfulness despite judgment and exile. We have other stories about all creation and the whole of human life reflecting God's wisdom, like the one in Proverbs this morning. These are stories that show how our Trinitarian God came to be known.

Our God is no remote heavenly power, no cosmic version of this or that strong man of history writ horribly large. Rather, our God's story is a counter-story, a liberating story, reaching its revolutionary zenith with the carpenter from Nazareth who loved and saved and confronted, who was done to death by the keepers of privilege and the guardians of decency. But God's counter-story continued in raising this Jesus from the dead, and releasing the Spirit of God's creative, liberating love in the community that Jesus gathered. This is the Spirit of Christ guiding us into all truth, as John says, forming Christ's mind in us and making us Christ's own legacy from God. In this story Christians can truly boast, as Paul puts it in that magnificent passage from Romans this morning. There the story of our suffering and disappointment is at the same time God's story, as God joins us in the far country of our human journeying, embracing the human struggle in all its bitterness. The cross of Jesus Christ stands at the heart of our story of God as Trinity, and the experience in Christ of God's own Spirit poured out on us.

Not a remote God, then, but a God who draws us into God's own life, urging us to boast, as Paul does today, that as we have access to the grace of God in Jesus Christ through the Holy Spirit. This mysticism of liberation and hope is the concrete experience of all who love and tell and are shaped by the long story of our God, whose rich and complex dealings with us have left us at last with this brief formula: "one God in three persons". This God reaches out with arms of love to entwine and win our hearts – in baptism when our lives are formally placed into the heart of God's love for us, and in every Eucharist, which mystically invites us into the life of God while at the same time propelling us out into the life of God's world.

At first, I didn't appreciate what was behind the simple, time-honoured phrases that people used to describe their loved ones who'd died. But in time I came to realise that beyond the familiar forms of words, a long and detailed story was being honoured – a story of love and faithfulness, no less deeply felt for being conventionally expressed. So it is, friends, with our faith in God the Holy Trinity. A living story of God's involvement with us and our ancestors in faith stands behind this familiar theological formula. And in our Eucharist today, as ever, this story of God opens out to welcome us, drawing us in, then sending us out into the world.

The Lord be with you...

Growing in the Womb of Love

Trinity Sunday, 12 June 2022, Year C,
St Philip's, O'Connor

Proverbs 8:1-4, 22-31; Psalm 8; Romans 5:1-5; John 16:12-15

✝ In the Name of the Father and of the Son and of the Holy Spirit. Amen.

A good friend of mine, whose name you'd know if I told it to you, says that he likes to talk with me about matters of faith, about the nature and content of Christian belief, and about how to understand passages in the Bible. Because, when he tries to talk to his parish priest and asks him the sort of questions that he asks me, very quickly the answer comes back "it's a mystery". I'm sure that this is the answer he'd get to the question about why we believe in God as Trinity: "it's a mystery".

But that's never how it's worked, really. The Trinity was something that people of faith worked out in the Church's early days. They were worshippers of Almighty God, the God of the Old Testament, yet they were bowled over by Jesus, crucified and risen, who *institutes* the nurturing habitat that the Holy Spirit *constitutes*.

So, the Trinity isn't just a mystery, if that means a conundrum. Instead it's a mystery of love, of belonging, a surprising discovery that we're alive to God in Jesus Christ, who's a going concern within and among us. I like the way that Scots theologian James Mackey frames the Trinitarian mystery. He says that the Trinity is our answer to the question: what sort of God do we meet in the story of Jesus Christ? So, instead of a remote something-or-other God, a revered teacher called Jesus who comes to mind occasionally, and a Spirit or a spirituality that might be just a benign sense of contentment – or of smug contentment – the Trinity is about something altogether more integral, more organic, more deeply personal.

The Church has often used images to evoke the Trinity, from St Patrick's three-leafed clover to Augustine's three dimensions of the human mind to today's imagery of God the Trinitarian pattern of human unity in diversity. Here's a new image from me, that you might like: we live and grow in the womb of God the Father; we're joined to God the Father by the nurturing umbilical cord of Jesus Christ, making us part of God's own life; and we're held safe in the preserving amniotic fluid of the Spirit, which is also God's substance and God's presence. This is an image of God for us: God transcending us yet enfolding us; the God that Jesus Christ reveals as our God; and God the Holy Spirit who provides the habitat for our creatureliness, in whose warm bath we become who God is making us. Not three functions, then, but one God and one coherent mission, one formative movement in three kinds of intimate embrace, yet all one reality, all one God, nothing of which we can leave out.

This Trinitarian God begins to peep out in the Old Testament. Proverbs today gives us God present in the wisdom that beckons and enlightens us, the same wisdom that reveals itself in the wonders of creation. This is God Almighty known at the same time as God nearby, God among, God involved, God responsible. Psalm 8, likewise, won't let us think of God's greatness without reminding us of God's nearness – the God *above us* who at the same time is God *for us*. In Romans today, Paul brings in Jesus Christ, describing him as our access to God, as God's justifying gift who enables us to grow through all challenges and suffering, thanks to the Spirit of this love and assurance that's given to us, which becomes our reliable standpoint. This early New Testament sensibility is already suggestive of the Trinity – the Father, the Son, and the Holy Spirit are all present. And you can't take any one of them away, or the Christian house of cards falls down.

Finally, in John's Gospel today, the Holy Spirit is presented as the context of our life in Christ, the bearer of Christ's life and of our share in God's promised future: God alongside us, God around us, God ahead of us.

So, friends, you can see in passages like this the coalescing spiritual vision of the earliest Churches, which was made formal in the age of the creeds: three persons, one God, ever to be worshipped and adored. And yes, it is a mystery, which requires unpacking and poetic evoking in every age. I've had my crack at that this morning, with my original image of our growing in the womb of God's love. Because, as my favourite theology teacher taught us back in student days, we need theology to point to mystery.

The Lord be with you ...

Corpus Christi

Beyond Sacrifice and Violence

Corpus Christi, Sunday 25 May 2008, Year A,
All Saints, Ainslie
Exodus 24:3-8; Psalm 116; 1 Corinthians 10:14-21; Matthew 14:12-26

† In the Name of the Father and of the Son and of the Holy Spirit. Amen.

None of us will have missed the major new phenomenon of reality television. Week by week, the clearly emotionally-damaged Gordon Ramsey sacrifices one of the young hopefuls in his TV restaurant *Hell's Kitchen*, with the connivance of other hopefuls who choose the victim – sacrificed to the dream they all share of having that final prize, their own restaurant. *Big Brother* and the *Survivor* series teach us to celebrate the values of competition and back-stabbing deception, also helping us get used to the idea that if you want to win the prizes you must be willing to do whatever the bosses say, however stupid and pointless. Hence the contestants become willing participants in a system that has contempt for them.

Does this sound familiar? Yes, it's the world we live in, where deep down so many people fear for their jobs and their mortgages, where keeping your head down and the boss happy are the two great commandments, and where we learn the lessons of me first and up-yours so effectively that many can't even do marriage and family any more. The global economy that takes no prisoners, the human resources management culture that treats people as expendable means rather than intrinsically worthwhile ends, and the increasing commodification of human beings into shopping drones and sexual objects – these are the idols of our society, before which a whole civilization uncomplainingly bows down and worships.

This weekend, as we celebrate the feast of Corpus Christi in the Eucharist, and the sacrament of baptism, we celebrate a different story, we dream a different dream, we take in a new set of values and priorities for life, beyond the idols that St Paul warns us about today, reminding us that in Jesus Christ we've moved on from them to something better.

Let me show you what I mean by reflecting with you on today's Gospel, which is full of meaning and hope for us. Our reading begins with a little fragment of the Gospel story that came before: 'His disciples came and took the body and buried it; then they went and told Jesus'. Whose body is this? Our Gospel reading today starts with yet another victim of the system, sacrificed to ego and ambition like so many others then and now. The body, of course, is John the Baptist, who was the unsuccessful contestant at King Herod's version of *Hell's Kitchen*, whose head was brought in on a platter. So, today's Gospel begins with a reminder of appalling horror and sacrificial violence. In the two scenes that follow, however, we see Jesus' answer to all this, and we're invited to imagine a world beyond the power of the idols.

As a response to Herod's awful banquet, and his vision of social life with human sacrifice as its acceptable price, Jesus puts on his own banquet in the wilderness, and he invites the multitude. As God his father had fed Israel in the desert, and made a covenant with his servant Moses – as we recalled in our first reading today – so Jesus recalls Israel to its founding dream of liberation, which is now his job to fulfil. Here there is plenty to go around and the community is knit together, totally unlike Herod's banquet, or more recent versions of it like *Big Brother* or *Survivor*, where everyone suspiciously eyes everyone else. Here is a foretaste of heaven, of the new creation and, as bread is broken for the renewal of human hope and belonging, here is a foretaste of the Eucharist.

In the next scene, the walking on the water, Jesus underlines the point by walking out to his frightened disciples in the boat – that is, in the Church. Water is the chaotic element, the symbol of violence and terror for ancient civilizations, so that overcoming its power is always a symbol of a new beginning in order and peace and hope – think of Noah's ark, the parting of the Red Sea at the Exodus and, placing this image right at the start of the Bible, God's Spirit moving on the face of the deep, to create a world of order and peace. Jesus likewise surmounts the chaos and terror of history to rescue and to reassure his people.

Now, we mustn't read this scene as first and foremost a miracle of buoyancy – just as we shouldn't read the feeding of the multitude as first and foremost a miracle of catering. These are highly symbolic stories with a forceful contemporary relevance. The scene of Jesus walking on the water uses hydrography to point to theology. Jesus overcomes the powers that limit and stifle human life, symbolised by the storm and the water. Just as Jesus challenges the construction of social order by repression and violence, symbolised by Herod's diabolical banquet, with a very different banquet of his own.

Friends, as our parish continues that meal with Jesus in our Eucharists this weekend, we also celebrate Jesus' triumph over the chaos of history, war and violence in baptism, where one of us is drowned in the deep waters of death with Jesus and rises to new life with him, sacramentally joined with him in his death and resurrection. And as *we* remember that our foreheads were marked with Jesus' cross in baptism, so we realise that we have been claimed for a different future, for a different agenda in life. Friends, you and I were marked in our baptism as people who don't have to play the game, who don't have to swallow the nonsense – the bullying rules of a system that dehumanises us, sacrificing others to our own ambition.

Perhaps we could register our protest at the dehumanising idols of this world by giving up the human sacrifice sort of reality television programs from today's date, because we've become aware from today's date of the new reality for which Jesus has claimed us. We may not become wealthy and successful if we choose to live the life of baptism and Eucharist, but when history is finally over and the truth is at last revealed, we'll know then who was on the winning side all the while.

The Lord be with you...

Body, Matter, Violence

Corpus Christi, Sunday 14 June 2020, Year A,
St Philip's, O'Connor

Exodus 24:3-8; Psalm 116; 1 Corinthians 10:14-21; Mark 4:12-26

✝ In the Name of the Father and of the Son and of the Holy Spirit. Amen.

Today, as we celebrate Corpus Christi, we reflect on God's gift of the Eucharist and on Jesus' presence in the bread and wine we receive – how Jesus' glorified body is given to us week by week as his Eucharistic body, which strengthens the Church to be his body in the world. Now, of course there are historical controversies around Christ's real presence in this sacrament. Militant Protestants reject it as much as militant Roman Catholics insist on it, and we might wonder whether Christ would recognise his presence in either extreme. As for Anglicans, we're characteristically ambivalent. Not many of us identify as Anglo-Catholic, as Fr Martin and I do, reflecting the influence of churches where our faith was nurtured from childhood. But even your more typically Protestant-minded Anglican recognises that the Eucharist is special, that there's a proper reverence in its celebration, that receiving communion is significant, and that the elements of bread and wine are to be treated respectfully. Mainstream Anglicans might not know why they have these instincts, but they do.

However, the Eucharist is too important for me to leave it at that, rehearsing historical controversies and defending Anglo-Catholic practices. The whole point of the Eucharist is bigger than Church traditions. It's about God's investment in all the heights and depths of human life, following the logic of the incarnation, and this has implications for Christian life in the real world. I'm going to mention three aspects: the Eucharist and today's widespread alienation from the human body; the Eucharist and our modern alienation from the material world, an alienation that lies behind the climate crisis; and, finally, the Eucharist in today's world of spiralling violence.

First, our body, the basis of whatever else we are as humans, is something that so many find themselves strangely alienated from. The body is displayed more than ever today, worshipped for its youth and beauty, eroticised like never before, sculpted by obsessive exercise; it's pierced and tattooed as a matter of course, too, so that our shifting identities across a lifetime are inked and punctured into it, making our body the museum of our memories and aspirations. Our bodies become curated objects, posed on Instagram in response to Instagram role models. Or else they become physical wrecks through the harmful things we do to them and put into them – the alienation of spirit that we inflict on them.

Those gripped by today's rising tide of gender dysphoria experience their bodies as hateful prisons of alienation, as places of exile. Likewise, the demand of new life given through the body becomes an unbearable burden, with some women concluding that their pregnant body has turned into the enemy of their freedom, of their identity. And so, at a time when you might conclude that the body has come into its own, instead it has widely become an object of estrangement, and on the basis of that alienation we form alienated relationships with other bodies.

But then one of us humans steps forward with enough self-possession to be able to offer his body to God and to us in the last supper and on the cross: "This is my body, given for you". In the face of Jesus we see humanity come right, and in the sacrament of Jesus' body and blood our own embodied life with all its physicality, all its potential, all its joys and its pains, its strange and persistent animality, is embraced by God and drawn by the Holy Spirit to its fulfilment. Friends, the Eucharist shows just how seriously God wants to love and heal us in our bodies, at a time when we seem especially bad as a civilization at doing that ourselves.

Now to my second point. What's true of the body in particular is true of material reality in general. Modern people can't imagine that Christ would or could come to us veiled in the forms of bread and wine, just as they can't imagine that the dead Jesus might be raised up by God from the brutal verdict of history on Good Friday to world-transforming life in the Holy Spirit on Easter Sunday. And this unimaginative, theological impoverishment spawns real-world consequences. As these doubts about the Eucharist grew in the early modern West, so we became progressively more alienated from the material world – more dominating and exploitative in our science, technology and industry; more prone to regard a world of things as merely resources and commodities. And with this came our continuing insensitivity to indigenous people and their integral belonging to country, to land and water and plants and wildlife.

I suggest that our colonial era excesses, and nowadays our obsession with resource extraction and maximising profits for the already rich, show a profound corruption of the sacramental imagination. Instead of being able to see Christ in the material world – in the faces of saints, in the holiness of sacred places, and pre-eminently in the bread and wine of the Eucharist – the only sacrament that anyone believes in today is money, which offers the only real presence worth celebrating.

My third point is that this anti-sacramental world is a dog-eat-dog world, a violent world, as ego and rivalry destroy community in country after country. But our Gospel today gives us an alternative. Notice that Jesus gathers his disciples for their last supper in the context of imminent betrayal from Judas. And notice, too, how Paul in our Epistle today sets Christians and their Eucharist against the world of pagan idolatry, which of course is a world of violent blood sacrifice. The Eucharist doesn't mean spiritual escape from a world of human ugliness and sinfulness, but, instead, it constitutes Christ's continuing self-giving in the midst of that world. The Eucharist isn't a pious denial of the Church's crimes and failures, either – remember, Judas was a communicant at that first Eucharist, and Jesus didn't refuse him. Because only Jesus' loving self-giving, over and over again, has a chance of challenging and breaking and hence changing human hearts – of defeating the pagan violence of our world with the force of love.

So, friends, for a humanity weakened in its resolve and its hope, in the grip of violence and alienation, the Eucharist is like a blood transfusion. The real presence of a healthier body is taken into our unhealthy bodies to enable their healing, their transformation. And not just our individual bodies but Christ's body, the Church. And, through Christ's abiding in his Church, his influence passes on to the body politic, and to better treatment of the natural world. You can call this mystical, you can call it political, but above all it's personal: Christ in person, given for us and to us. It's not hocus pocus, but God's continuing self-investment in the world that God loves, with Christ taken not just into our hearts and minds, but into our hands, our mouths, our bodies.

The Lord be with you ...

Mary

Something's Missing

St Mary the Virgin (transferred), Sunday 19 August 2012,
All Saints, Ainslie

Isaiah 61:10-62:3; Psalm 113; Galatians 4:4-7; Luke 2:1-7

✝ In the Name of the Father and of the Son and of the Holy Spirit. Amen.

I want to share with you today a sense of disappointment and loss that I feel as a Christian who lives separated from the Church of Rome and the great Orthodox Churches of the East. The Protestant resistance to Mary, which is shared by much of Anglicanism, is something that saddens me, but it also points to an absence that I feel in myself. Unlike me, I know that many Catholic and Orthodox Christians experience Mary as a living personal reality, as the mother of their saviour who remains close to them throughout life – whose love for Jesus and for all those who follow him is something that they *feel*.

One of my favourite theological writers, Fr James Alison, grew up in an Evangelical Anglican household but converted to Roman Catholicism as a young adult. One of the things that surprised him was that he developed a personal relationship with Mary, who became a living icon of God's loving face turned towards him in welcome. None of the urgent Protestant emphasis on personal assurance of salvation had ever gotten through to James as he was growing up, but in Mary he came to find this assurance in an intimate way.

Many other Catholic priests and monks vowed to chastity find in Mary a reassuringly feminine side to God. She helps them to be psychologically and sexually whole people, so that as disciplined celibates they can nevertheless bring gifts of warmth and vulnerability and intimacy to the task of pastoral care and friendship, and to find support in what can be a long and lonely calling.

As an Anglican, with my eye always on the Bible, I know that Mary has several appearances and many resonances in Scripture. We catch a foretaste of her in Isaiah today, for instance. It's hard to read that text about faithful Israel and the calling of its prophets and not think of Mary. In Galatians today, Paul emphasises the importance of Jesus' birth from a woman, under the same constraints that bind all of us – and indeed Church history teaches that the main reason Mary came to be called Mother of God is because this title helped to emphasise the humanity that Jesus shared with us. And then there's today's Gospel, when the might and power of Rome's Empire and its leaders is gently sidelined, in favour of God's new action among the humble and powerless who Mary represents. In her Magnificat, God's judgment is revealed as the mighty are cast down from their seats, exalting the humble and meek. So, the pious plaster statue version of Mary gives way, replaced in the Bible by a revolutionary virgin who announces God's coming reign.

As an Anglican, too, I know the violent history of English resistance to Roman Catholic claims under the Tudors and the Stuarts. Marian devotion was radically repressed in England, leaving only two sober mentions of her, with two bland collects, in *The Book of Common Prayer* – for Mary's birth, which we observe today, and for her Annunciation. So, when Anglo-Catholics brought back statues of Mary into our Church, and when they began to pray the Rosary, as I sometimes do, it was inevitably an act of protest against the Church of England's anti-Roman obsessions. A lot of Anglo-Catholicism loves to be a bit naughty, after all. Introducing Marian devotion into Anglican life is a bit like bringing a racy new girlfriend home to our rather straitlaced family for Sunday lunch.

As an Anglo-Catholic, I can even make theological sense out of the Roman Church's Marian dogmas – the immaculate conception, which declares Mary to have been conceived without taint of original sin, and her assumption into heaven. These dogmas, made official in the 1870s and the 1950s respectively, testify to Mary never having been separated from her divine son – not in her life on earth, not at its beginning, not at its end, and not in heaven. Mary preserved inviolate and inseparable from her son in this world and the next is a lovely Gospel idea, even if we know that these controversial claims also served a political purpose for the Roman Catholic Church, reasserting its flagging authority in the teeth of modern secularism and scepticism. Lovely ideas nonetheless – not strictly biblical, but not wildly unbiblical either, I like to think.

So, I'm an enthusiast for Mary, but I find it hard to access that enthusiasm outside my head – outside the realm of theological ideas. I haven't been trained at the knee of a Catholic mother to know Mary through prayer and to trust her deep in my heart – not an alternative to her son, certainly, but just as certainly a central player in the drama of faith to which her son has invited us.

Perhaps this personal disappointment that I feel – honouring Mary in my head and in my devotion though not really knowing her in my lived experience – is one of the salutary pains to be borne as a sign of our broken, divided Church. There are some things that we Anglicans have that Roman Catholics and the Orthodox struggle to find – a strong sense of lay authority, for instance, with a capacity to embrace the modern world and live with its moral ambiguity. But there are some things that we Anglicans miss in being separated from the great Church of the West, not to mention the great Churches of the East. And one of them is this sense of Mary as our intimate friend and a precious gift to us from her son.

So I suggest that we might begin thinking of Mary as a relative we didn't know we had – as a long-lost mother, perhaps, or, to shift the image, as a wonderful soul friend we have yet to meet – but if we did meet her, she'd be a great enrichment to our lives. Rather than a threat to the all-sufficiency of Christ, we might think of Mary as Jesus' first and best witness, helping to knit his life together inside us, as God knit Jesus' life together inside her.

Hail Mary, full of grace, the Lord is with you. Blessed are you among women, and blessed is the fruit of your womb, Jesus. Amen.

Our Long-Lost Half-Sister

Feast of the Assumption, 15 August 2013,
St Peter's, Eastern Hill, Melbourne
Revelation 11:19a; 12:1-6a, 10; Psalm 45;
1 Corinthians 15:20-26; Luke 1:39-56

✝ In the Name of the Father and of the Son and of the Holy Spirit. Amen.

It's a privilege to be with you tonight in this great Anglo-Catholic shrine for an evening of worship, fellowship, and reflection on the odd-sounding theme of Evangelical Catholicism, and I thank Fr Hugh the Vicar for his invitation. To help get us into the mood, I'm going to make a perverse attempt at interpreting Marian dogma as a testimony to Evangelical truth. Why? Because I think that Mary's Glorious Assumption, like her Immaculate Conception, takes us to the very heart of what the Gospel means for us.

But to begin, let me name the strangeness and even awkwardness that Anglicans typically feel about Mary. Her feast days were not entirely removed from *The Book of Common Prayer* by that increasingly convinced Protestant Cranmer, but her cult and personal devotion to Mary are things that few if any Anglicans learn at their mother's knee. Nevertheless, the majority of Christians, both Roman Catholic and Orthodox, know Mary as a personal reality and they talk to her, not just about her – they believe her to be so caught up in the life of Christ and his heavenly Father that where they are she too must surely be.

I'm reminded here of my own experience, twenty years ago now, of having an adoption reunion with my natural mother, and subsequently with my natural father and his family. It turned out that I have two half-sisters who I didn't know about, and to meet them was to learn new things about myself. Kim and Jo were young, fit and feisty – Tony Abbott would add that they had sex appeal! They were talkative, funny, and athletic. Kim was an *equestrienne* and Jo was a champion kayaker, which helped me realise that I had it in me to be a much more physical person than I'd previously imagined.

One night, after a few drinks and a few laughs we got our shoes off and discovered with delight that for each of us, like our father, our first three toes were all the same length. These strangers were becoming friends. I resembled them; I discovered that I liked them, and that they liked me. I tell you this story because it's the same for Anglicans with Mary, our beautiful, fascinating half-sister who many of us didn't know that we had. So perhaps it's worth getting to know Mary better, and to make a place for her in our Anglican family story.

Now, the Evangelical will seek biblical warrant for this suggestion, and rightly, and we can I think provide it. Our lectionary readings tonight are a good start.

Our Revelation passage features the figure of a woman who might be Israel or who might be the Church, or both, but she's also *prima facie* the figure of Mary, the mother of a child whose struggle for our salvation is being set out in rich allegory. This woman is presented here as central to the mystery of the Church, as the Second Vatican Council also reminds us, and her figure crowned with stars is there for us to meditate on with the other glorious mysteries of the Holy Rosary. But these developed convictions and practices draw on the Scripture. Consider, too, our 1 Corinthians passage tonight, where Christ risen is the first fruits of a bumper harvest, with the emphasis on our share as Christians in Christ's victory. It's precisely here that the tradition locates Mary, as the first among those who are redeemed by her son.

In our gospel tonight, Mary serves as a kind of hinge in salvation history. In Advent, we focus both on John the Baptist and Mary as the forerunners of Christ, but while John the Baptist is less than the least in the new covenant, and only points with his long finger across the gap between the testaments to Christ, Mary crosses that gap from the Old Covenant to the New – not least in the Magnificat, drawn from the songbook of Israel to take its place of honour in the Church's songbook. Likewise, Mary's status as blessed among women is revealed in the Holy Spirit to Elizabeth, who leads the praise of Mary in her generation to which new voices are added in every subsequent generation, including ours tonight.

All these readings point to being caught up in Christ's purposes and in his salvation, and in two of them Mary stands centrally. She is integral not only to the mystery of the Church but to that of our salvation itself – not as its agent, as the Protestants rightly fear, but as a participant leading the way into Christ for the rest of us who follow. Catholic theologian Fr James Alison develops this idea, clearly with the concerns of Evangelicals in mind. "This is", he writes,

> the maximum declaration of God's victory in Christ, and a sign of the shape of that victory. Of course, the victory was won, the battle was over, the moment that heaven became forever a human story when Christ ascended to the right hand of God, taking a human nature, meaning a lived-out human story, to be the paradigm of heaven. But the fullness of the shape of that victory only really becomes clear with the Assumption into heaven of our Lady and her Coronation. That is when it becomes quite luminous not merely that we have been saved, but what it is that has been saved and what it looks like to be saved.[10]

Here we're close to understanding the mystery of the Church and its saints, and of the Eucharist as well. The reality of Christ becomes the primary reality of the Church and the Christians of

---

10 James Alison, "Living the Magnificat", in *Broken Hearts and New Creations: Intimations of a Great Reversal* (London and New York: Continuum, 2010), 17-33, at 23.

which he is the first fruits, the head united with its members, just as Christ who gives himself with the bread and wine of the last supper becomes the deepest reality of these gifts. So, we're not allowed as Christians to think of ourselves apart from Christ's transforming love for us – apart from Christ as the chief truth about the people that baptism has made us. Nor are we as Catholic Christians able to think of the Eucharistic bread and wine apart from Christ's gift of himself, which they most truly are.

By the same salvific, ecclesial and sacramental logic, we can no longer think of Mary apart from Christ – neither at her end, in her glorious Assumption and Coronation, where she is ahead of us yet still at one with us; nor at her beginning, in her Immaculate Conception, which testifies that Christ was always at the heart of Mary's life. As James Alison's Dominican teacher, Fr Herbert McCabe, put it, "the doctrine of the Immaculate Conception says that the Holy Spirit did not just come down upon Mary out of the blue at the Annunciation, it was the culmination of a coming of the Spirit in Mary that was from the beginning, from the roots of her existence".[11]

This is what I'm calling the Evangelical logic of Marian dogma – of the Glorious Assumption, but also the Immaculate Conception – in which we see fleshed out the transforming claim of Christ on the being of a person, down to their roots; likewise, what we see confirmed in advance with Mary's Assumption and what *we will ourselves confirm*, albeit in arrears, when our own share in Christ's resurrection is finally revealed, and with it the truth of our lives held precious in Christ, right from the time of our own conception.

But if I can declare an Evangelical logic concerning Mary, based on her share in the life of Christ, I think we can also share in Evangelical joy. James Alison points out that Marian devotion always brings joy and festivity in Catholic circles. Raised as an

---

11 Herbert McCabe OP, "The Immaculate Conception" in *God Matters* (1987) (London and New York: Continuum, 2010), 210-14, at 213.

Anglican Evangelical, he was converted to Catholicism at least in part because in Mary he found what Evangelical claims for assurance of salvation had failed to bring him: a sense of heaven bending to meet us in reassurance. "So", as he writes, "the adventure is not one of tragic heroism but is a much safer story than we can normally dare to believe. After all, salvation that didn't come with an expansive sense of safety wouldn't be worth it".[12]

This is a salutary reminder to us personally, but also as a Church. The joy and the freedom of the Gospel ought to be something that both Evangelicals and Anglo-Catholics radiate, but too often our Church is more about duty than delight, more about dogged perseverance than celebration, more of an ordeal than a blessing, and increasingly more of a managed institution than a spiritual movement – besides which we're now being subjected to excoriating public analysis by Royal Commissions, so that our many failings have helped make the Church the scapegoat-in-chief for today's legion of detractors. Whereas, for James Alison, Mary's song of joy in the Magnificat provides a corrective boost to our flagging spirits, reminding us, as he memorably puts it, that "whatever may be the immediate appearances, we are in much more of a playground and much less of a war zone than we are inclined to think".[13]

So, friends, here is the Evangelical Catholicism that Mary brings us, our beautiful if unfamiliar or even unknown half-sister who is nevertheless like us, who is one of us, who simply likes us, and who wants us to talk to her – whose love for us and solidarity with us is constantly being expressed before God's face in heaven. Getting to know my own half-sisters, I came to understand myself better and feel better about myself. I suggest that the same can be true for Anglicans as we discover and get to know Mary.

The Lord be with you....

---

12 Alison, "Living the Magnificat", 25.
13 Alison, "Living the Magnificat", 33.

St Michael and All Angels
(Michaelmas)

Angels?

St Michael and All Angels, Sunday 28 September 2008,
All Saints', Ainslie

Daniel 7:9-10; Psalm 138; Revelation 12:7-12a; John 1:45-51

✝ In the Name of the Father and of the Son and of the Holy Spirit. Amen.

Very truly, I tell you, you will see heaven opened and the angels of God ascending and descending upon the Son of Man. (John 1:51)

Who would have thought – twenty-five years ago – that bottled water would become popular, and that people would make a fortune selling it? In the same way, I couldn't have predicted twenty-five years ago as a first-year theological student – convincing myself that angels were a figment of ancient imagination, a bit of biblical mythology – that angels would come back with such a vengeance as a major cultural phenomenon. Angels are big in films and television, big in children's fiction and big in merchandising, and not just religious merchandising. Angels are everywhere in pendants and ornaments, in jewellery and pictures, and up there with dolphins and crystals in the new age spiritual firmament. Clearly some deep nerve is being touched in this pop-culture phenomenon, and I'll be offering a few thoughts about that this morning, and about how we Christians might view today's whole angel resurgence. But first a bit of background. Where did the idea of angels come from, and what did angels mean for the Bible and the tradition?

The angels were originally the host of heaven in ancient Near-Eastern cosmology, and we find echoes of this in the Old

Testament. Wherever we see morning stars singing together and heavenly courts, like the heavenly court in our Daniel reading today, we see the religious imagination of the ancient Near East being taken up and made part of the Bible's vision. Ancient Near-Eastern dualism, with forces of light and darkness locked forever in combat also involves angels, and our Revelations reading this morning, with Michael and the heavenly angels defeating Satan and his angels, recalls the basic metaphysics of conflict that ancient Israel encountered among the nations it colonised. So, the Bible took these local cultures seriously, but not on their own terms.

The angels become the heavenly court of the God of Israel, the God of the covenant, the God of human beings, our God. And the cosmic conflict of ancient Babylonian dualism doesn't become a struggle of equals for the Bible but, rather, a complete rout of evil by good, in which there's no real contest. Our God rules the cosmic roost, and all the things that went bump in the night throughout antiquity are kept on a very short lead in God's world, according to the Old Testament.

Angels became messengers of God in the Old Testament, signs of God's presence in God's world. God may be high and lifted up, but the world is still charged with the glory and presence of God. This fundamental paradox of the Judaeo-Christian imagination – that the high God is also the world-loving, world embracing God, our God and the God of our children – is a paradox that angels helped the biblical writers to imagine. Angels appear at many key moments in the Old Testament, with news or action from God.

So, while the angels were taken over from the religions of the ancient Near East by the Bible, they were adapted to serve the Old Testament religious vision. And this remains true in the New Testament. Angels were part of the religious imagination of Jesus, and of his followers who wrote the New Testament. They're written into the story as messengers at all the key points of Jesus' life, and as heralds of his resurrection. Once or twice in the New Testament angels are mentioned as guardians. And they represent the unseen powers controlling life and history, where we read about angels of the churches and angels of the nations. We try to understand affairs today in terms of psychological, cultural and economic forces. The idea of angels served the same purpose for New Testament writers, with their "powers and principalities in the heavenly places".

But the key thing about angels in the New Testament is the way that they're rigorously marshalled as witnesses to Jesus. His annunciation, his birth and his resurrection are proclaimed by angels, and according to 1 Peter his gospel is something into which angels long to look. Jesus' incarnation makes him for a time lower than the angels, according to the prologue of Hebrews, but at last he will be set high above them as their Lord. The struggle of Michael and the angels against evil in today's Revelations reading is a powerful image of the triumph of Jesus himself and of his gospel over evil, which God won for us through Jesus' cross and resurrection. And in today's Gospel – recalling Jacob's dream at Bethel in Genesis 28 – we have the loveliest New Testament reference to angels and their proper place in Christian faith.

As Jacob dreamed at Bethel and saw a ladder set up on the earth, with angels ascending and descending, so John's Jesus annexes this story and applies it to himself in today's Gospel. Wherever Jesus is, we find a ladder set up between heaven and earth, and in our imagination we can see angels ascending and descending upon the son of man. That is, in Jesus Christ, we can see the distance between God and human beings bridged once and for all; in Jesus Christ, the divine-human one, we can see all the traffic between earth and heaven, between heaven and earth, re-routed. In Jesus Christ, every cry and yearning of the human heart is taken up to heaven, and every tender, resolute intention of God toward you and toward me is brought down to earth. Today's Gospel is an imaginative witness to the centrality of Jesus for Christian faith and imagination, with a God who is very near to us.

But the story doesn't end there. In the middle ages, Christians imagined a great cosmology, a multi-layered universe, chock full of divine presence, with so many angels there was no limit to how many could fit even on the head of a pin. This popular illustration isn't logic splitting so much as religious imagination. The world is charged with the glory of God. The universe is a rich, teeming and complementary whole, with angels and humans each having their place – "ordained and constituted in a wonderful order", as our traditional collect for today so beautifully puts it. And we see something of this medieval cosmic order in today's first hymn, with the nine angelic choirs of medieval imagination all named for us: "bright seraphs, cherubim and thrones", there's the top three, and then six more: "dominions, princedoms, powers, virtues, archangels, angels' choirs". And, of course, in verse two of the hymn the Queen of Heaven, the Blessed Virgin Mary, the "bearer of the eternal word, most gracious", makes her appearance at the apex of the medieval religious imagination, portrayed in the hymn as "higher than the cherubim, more glorious than the seraphim".

Yet as we know, this rich cosmic tapestry, this medieval vision splendid, broke down. From the seventeenth century, science gave us instead a mechanical cosmos, ruled by rational, inviolate physical laws. Even the great physicist Isaac Newton needed angels to keep planets from wobbling in his not-quite perfect theory, but Pierre Simon de Laplace got the mathematics right, and the angels were made gravitationally redundant. Instead of a rich, teeming Catholic cosmos, we were left with a rational, ordered, planned and manageable Protestant cosmos, and hence the imaginative scope of today's democratic capitalist world emerged. Angels came to be seen as part of the history of ideas and not the furniture of the universe, as John Macquarrie put it.

But many hated this spiritually-evacuated modern Enlightenment vision and protested against it. German idealism recovered a sense of the divine spirit in history, and in Marxism we find an enormously influential secular echo of that belief. But chiefly I think of the Romantic movement, which preferred imagination over information, and sentiment over science. Angels rushed back in Romantic writing and art, and in the pre-Raphaelite painters we see a particularly rich, nostalgic, imaginative attempt to recapture the medieval world in which human beings could feel at home and not like isolated atoms bouncing about in a void, as the Enlightenment vision seemed to prefer it. This romantic, nostalgic, sentimental spirit found other nineteenth-century expressions, too – in the arts and crafts movement, in neo-gothic architecture and in Anglo-Catholic ritualism. And it survives as a major protest movement in our culture today, as more and more people in our technological, information age opt for a more or less magical view of life and reality.

Which brings me back to the resurgence of angels in today's Western cultural imagination. Part of it is the continuing influence of Romanticism, which I understand as a protest movement against domination by scientific rationality. Many people can't bear an unsparing secular vision, a spiritually neutral world, with human beings on their own before a vast and uncomprehending cosmos.

Yet another factor, a new twist, is the deregulation of spirituality. God may have died as the major unifying idea of Western culture, as late as the 1960s, but spirituality is alive and well. It's just become deregulated, around the same time as our economies in the West were deregulated. God went the way of the gold standard, yet the angels float free, as our currencies and exchange rates do. Iris Murdoch signalled this cultural shift of mood in her 1966 novel *The Time of the Angels*, in which the death of conventional religious belief unleashes a flood of deregulated spiritual sensibility, symbolised by angels. A world full of angels is what today's imagination has put in place of yesterday's clear and well-integrated belief in God, and in Jesus Christ.

But there are still further aspects of the reappearance of angels in contemporary culture. There's the fear of cosmic aloneness, so that angels recall the richly populated medieval cosmos for anxious, post-modern urban westerners with our single occupancy apartments and our flexible families. And as well as angels, of course, we have extra-terrestrials, who nearly everybody seems to believe in, and who regularly have lots of Americans over for a visit, if daytime television can be believed. Whether or not there are actual angels, or actual extra-terrestrials for that matter, the idea of them has come to function as a cultural necessity, otherwise the universe would be too bleak and empty.

And here's another contributing factor. Our Western culture today is recovering a sense of holism, beyond isolated atoms bumping about in a rule-governed void. We've learned about chaos theory, for instance, and the deep interconnectedness of everyday phenomena. We've come to a much more systemic vision of the forces that shape our lives, and so we want to be less individualistic, more environmentally conscious, more holistic. This is a good thing, and closer to the Trinitarian vision, favouring mutuality and belonging over isolated individualism. So, in a more open universe, science itself becomes more open to complexity, to uncertainty, to mystery – even to spirituality, as a slew of science and spirituality books shows, ever since Fritjoff Capra wrote *The Tao of Physics* in 1975.

So, angels returning with a vengeance in our popular culture points to a new spiritual holism but also to a new a spiritual yearning in the post-modern West. Whether or not angels exist, I sense that we Christians can still deploy the idea of them as we always have in the Bible and the tradition. But as we celebrate the angels, and their ministry, we who celebrate them are Christians, not new age westerners who love the diversity of spiritualities today but who can't hold on to the unity, to the deep purpose, which we Christians see undergirding our lives and our whole cosmos.

As we commemorate St Michael and all Angels, we celebrate in the spirit of the Bible, which employs angels as witnesses to God's glory, to God's embrace of us and our world, and to the one in whom heaven and earth, humans and God, are definitively joined, our Lord Jesus Christ: because "Very truly, I tell you, you will see heaven opened and the angels of God ascending and descending upon the Son of Man".

The Lord be with you...

All Singing, All Dancing

St Michael and All Angels, 27 September 2015,
All Saints', Ainslie

Daniel 7:9-10, 13-14; Psalm 138; Revelation 12:7-12a; John 1:45-51

✝ In the Name of the Father and of the Son and of the Holy Spirit. Amen.

If your life was a TV show or a movie, a play or a stage show, what sort would it be? Would it be a one man or one woman show, with you and your talent against the world? Would it be one of those tortured plays by Chekhov or films by Ingmar Bergman – the sort that a younger Woody Allen loved to make fun of? Would you be in a reality TV show, fighting it out in a kitchen or struggling through some physical ordeal – all cut-throat competition and humiliation in front of a hungry audience? Would it be one of those glib crime shows meant to gloss over the horrors of life? Or would it be something more serious, like Scandinavian noir or *House of Cards*, where no-one can be trusted and where cynicism wins the day?

Friends, the type of drama we imagine ourselves caught up in shapes who we are. It provides the script that we follow in life. But if our role is as a loser, a victim, a bully, a bore, a pain in the neck, an overachiever, a serial self-saboteur, that role *can* be changed for the better *if* we can start to imagine things differently. What if we Christians are caught up in a drama that's quite different from the one that we've grown used to? What if the show is grander, richer, funnier, more moving, more hopeful, more joyful, with a great big finish with everyone on stage including all those who've been lost along the way? What if the Christian life is best understood as being part of a grand, lavish, all-singing, all-dancing musical? What if our individual challenges and relationship conflicts, our setbacks and dark moments suddenly change their character, as the music swells, as a cramped scene opens out to reveal a new vista, and as a whole cast of new characters suddenly comes on stage? The familiar words and struggles of normal life give way to new scenes and possibilities, to rejoicing and movement – it's the same life, but a life that's now crucially different.

All this is what we're doing today as we celebrate Michaelmas, the Feast of St Michael and All Angels. Today we came in the door as individuals or couples or families but suddenly we're part of one of Catholic Christianity's great festivals of the imagination, with angels and archangels and the whole company of heaven. Our normal, regular, familiar world, the world of rationality, prudence, and modest expectations, gives way. Instead, it's as if we're transported to the golden years of Hollywood, with a studio orchestra, with big choreographed dance numbers, with chorus girls – and, of course, with synchronised swimming! The universe that we might think belonged to the likes of Stephen Hawking and to the property developers, is rediscovered as a spiritual place, alive with God's presence, with God's loving energy, with God's claim mediated through innumerable angels. These angels who represent God's compassion towards us and lift up God's glorious praise even when we Christians are discouraged and preoccupied.

The Holy Angels are one of the Bible's ways of imagining God's presence, God's influence, and God's care for the people of God. Our first reading today, from the book of Daniel, gives us this very vision, with "one like a human being" coming on the clouds of heaven. This is a vision of humanity judged and liberated, of humanity lifted up to God as all the injustices of history are put right at last. God's claim on humanity is fulfilled in a great final production number that's as liturgical as it is political. This is a dominion and glory and kingship that will never pass away.

In our second reading, from the Book of Revelation, we have another imaginative vision: of human history as God's victorious struggle against evil and folly in which you and I have a share.

Our human struggles are projected onto a cosmic canvas, with Michael the Archangel defeating Satan – that is, with Jesus Christ overcoming every evil that bedevils us, to which the whole creation resounds in grateful thanks.

And, as with every appearance of Angels in the New Testament, the message is driven home that they belong to Jesus now, revealing his message and serving his cause. Whatever anyone in the ancient world might have thought about angels, or indeed in our modern world where free-range angels are popular with the friends of dolphins and the crystal gazers, the New Testament angels work for Jesus.

All this helps us to understand today's gospel. As in a musical, an ordinary conversation between Philip and Nathaniel, then between Nathaniel and Jesus, suddenly changes. A wider scene is revealed, so that suddenly what was personal and earthbound, what was a matter of faith and belief, suddenly reveals a whole new, larger, cosmic context: "You will see greater things than these", Jesus declares; "Very truly, I tell you, you will see heaven opened and the angels of God ascending and descending upon the Son of Man" (John 1:51). Can you imagine a big scene from a show like *Jesus Christ Superstar*, or *Godspell*, with Jesus on a stairway to heaven surrounded by angels streaming up and down at his bidding? This is the very point. Jesus Christ is our guaranteed human connection to heaven and Jesus Christ is heaven's unbreakable bond with us, so that in Jesus Christ all the traffic between God the Father and humanity flows reliably and unceasingly.

The point of all this is so that you and I can take comfort, take heart, and recover our bearings in life. The Psalmist this morning sings in thankfulness to God, who hears us, who answers us, who looms over kings to care for the lowly, and who will never let us go. This Feast of St Michael and All Angels offers earthbound, jaded and beleaguered Christian imaginations something quite unexpected. The tragic drama or the unrewarding slog of so many lives suddenly looks more like a Hollywood musical; the serious documentary that we're plodding through suddenly reveals a chorus line, with everybody on stage to celebrate.

Today, we rejoice in a vision of heaven's great company bent towards us in loving embrace, which is never more the case than here in the Eucharist. Here, we imagine angels, archangels and the whole company of heaven veiling their faces as the Lord Jesus Christ comes again to earth in this Holy Sacrament – "as the light of light comes shining from the realms of endless day," which is how the ancient writer pictured it. Here in the Eucharist, the angels stand with us and sing God's praise with us, they pray with us and they pray *for us*. And why? Because the Holy Angels love us with the love of Jesus, whom they represent, and because they're on our side.

The Lord be with you...

All Saints' Day

The Saints: Role Models and More

All Saints' Day (transferred to 29 October 2011), Year A,
All Saints, Ainslie
Revelations 7:9-17; Psalm 34:1-10, 22;
1 John 3:1-3; Matthew 5:1-12

✝ In the Name of the Father and of the Son and of the Holy Spirit. Amen.

I once saw an interview with the owner of a private animal sanctuary in Victoria. He was a hard-bitten agnostic, but he'd set up a statue of Francis of Assisi on his property and he used to tell visiting school groups about the saint. "I can explain St Francis to a kid", he said, "but I can't explain God to myself"! No wonder people get into such a muddle about God. We talk about God as an unknowable mystery, and philosophers debate God's existence as if it can be settled by clever arguments. But our Christian understanding of God is not so remote; "God is Christlike, and in him is no un-Christ likeness at all", as Archbishop Michael Ramsey reminded us.

If God is a mystery, then, we mean a mystery of relationship, of loving inclusion, as Christ draws us into the mystery of God's inner life through the Holy Spirit. If God is unknowable, nevertheless we're still truly joined to God even though as to one unknown, as St Thomas Aquinas explained. So, if God seems incomprehensible and incredible and unlikely to many people, the Christian is content to point to Christ, and to those whom Christ joins to himself through the Holy Spirit. Here we can come to know God. Christ and his saints reveal God to be an inclusive personal reality rather than an abstract idea.

Now, who are the saints? For St Paul in his letters, it's very clear that all Christians are saints, caught up through their baptism into the life of Christ. This "everyday mysticism" is hard to make sense of for today's preoccupied, self-reliant sceptics – to see our lives in terms of belonging to Christ first and foremost. This emphasis represented the great rediscovery that was the Protestant Reformation: that we are God's children now, as our second reading reassures us. We don't have to make ourselves acceptable to God by our own good behaviour, which is what many people think – sadly, even many Protestants who should know better. And we only fail to understand this because the world doesn't understand God properly, as our second reading goes on to say. Many people think that God is their rival in life – that you can't truly be yourself, that you can't truly be free, if you're not able to do whatever you want. Many people think that God's will is weird, unnatural, and alien, with all those don'ts. William Blake spoke for all those people when he wrote,

And Priests in black gowns, were walking their rounds
And binding with briars, my joys & desires.[14]

But the vision of the New Testament – of Paul and of John in our Epistle today – is that serving God reveals who we most deeply are, and gives us the identity and freedom we crave: "what we know is this: when he is revealed we will be like him ..." (1 John 3:2). The atheists, who reject God, might be more open to Christian belief if they understood this.

"And all who have this hope in him purify themselves, as he is pure", as our second reading concludes. Here is the secret of being saints. It's about being called by God in baptism to a process

---

14 William Blake, "The Garden of Love", online at https://www.poetryfoundation.org/poems/45950/the-garden-of-love (last accessed August 2022).

of transformation, of mind and heart and will, through which we come into increasing alignment with God's own desire. The purity to which we're called isn't a fierce, morally superior posture of disapproving rectitude, either. Rather, it's Christ's purity, which is robust, humane, attractive and life-giving.

Now, as for you and me, this call, this invitation, is meant to issue in a range of new attitudes and behaviours. Our Gospel today contains a famous list of these, from Jesus' Sermon on the Mount. Here's how we recognise the blessed ones: they live with incredible freedom, because death no longer shuts down their imaginations. So, instead of hoarding and protecting what's ours, a whole new moral imagination becomes possible for us with the resurrection of Jesus. Those whom this Gospel calls poor in spirit and meek are simply those who know this gift and call from God and have been set free from a life of defending themselves, of big noting themselves, and of looking out for #1.

This also allows the poor in spirit, the meek, to be merciful while still yearning for God's righteousness, and for these two commitments not to be at odds. Righteousness often means no more than self-righteousness without room for mercy, because our anxious posture makes us into disapproving, judgmental people. On the other hand, there's a kind of mercy that makes no demands, that dreams no dreams of things being different. It's the slack moral posture of someone who doesn't want to have to confront anything in their own life. But in Jesus a deep hunger for goodness and justice is held together with merciful compassion, because both have the same roots in God's transforming love for us.

As a result, of course, these blessed ones are to some degree out of step with how things normally go in the world. They will be agents of God's peace; their purity will be an affront to evil people and evil systems, so that they will find themselves reviled and persecuted. As the German theologian Jürgen Moltmann put it, referring to Christians who resisted the Nazis, "they stood for the coming truth against the ruling lie". So, being caught up in

Jesus' life with God, and purifying ourselves as he is pure, is going to lead us with him along the road less travelled in life. And along this road, we find the shrines of the well-known saints, along with the murdered bodies of the martyrs.

Now, everything I've said so far would make sense both to a Protestant and to a Catholic. The Bible's teaching is quite clear to both: God makes us God's children through Jesus Christ, and in him we have the opportunity to be made more and more like Christ, if we accept the gift of grace that God freely gives us rather than turn against God in life. But divisions between Protestant and Catholic appear when it comes to the official saints of the Church. Both Catholic and Protestant are happy with the official saints as role models, helping us by their example to become more Christlike. But the Catholic Church always went further, and this extra dimension of Catholic teaching on the saints has made Protestants uneasy.

The Catholic saints enjoy the vision of God now while other departed Christians are still being made ready for that vision in purgatory. The Catholic saints saved up a store of benefits through their holy lives that can now be made available by the Church to help the rest of us on our way. Hence, we could pray for the merits of the saints to be applied to us – rather like the European Union bailing out the Greek economy. More generally, the Catholic vision sees the saints in heaven and on earth in unbroken relationship, so that we can direct our prayers to them, join our prayers with theirs, and know that they pray for us before the throne of grace.

All this is very disquieting for many Protestants, who insist that Christ alone is our mediator with God, that Christ alone is the meritorious one from whose actions we can benefit. Moreover, the whole idea of a heavenly industry dispensing grace through indulgences and Masses for the dead was opposed by the Protestant Reformers because it makes bureaucratic and institutional what should be direct and personal. Hence the strict ban on prayers for the dead in Protestant Churches, and on prayers to the Saints, and the particular suspicion of devotion to Mary, though on any scriptural reckoning she must surely be seen as first among Christians, forever blessed among women, and hence as Queen of the Saints.

Anglicans have tended to share the Protestant reserve regarding official saints. Yes, we kept days set apart for the saints in our prayer book, or at least the main New Testament ones, but the language of our authorised prayers on All Saints' Day goes no further than to honour them as good examples. Anglicans tend to prefer doing their spiritual business with God directly.

But in the Anglo-Catholic tradition, which many of us grew up in and some of us still think has some life in it, there's scope for joining a proper Protestant insistence on the all-sufficiency of Christ with the more lavish, more sprawling, more cosmic, and more ecclesial Catholic view of the Saints. As a Catholic-minded Anglican, I don't see the world in terms of spiritual individuals doing their private Christian business with God in company with the like-minded, with a small supply of saints available should we perhaps want them – like an ingredient we keep in the pantry that we may or may not need. Rather, I see the Church at the centre of Christian life, and our life with God as thoroughly collective, thoroughly mediated, thoroughly interdependent. And not just the Church on earth. We run our race before a great cloud of witnesses, as Hebrews 12 reminds us, and they're cheering for us. Like a football crowd, the company of heaven roars in delight at our triumphs in faith, hope and love, just as it groans with us in frustration when we mess up, because they're on our side.

I don't believe that God is an individual, either, just like us but only a lot bigger. Rather, I believe that while the life of God has a definite centre in Father, Son and Spirit, nevertheless it has an ever-widening circumference, into which you and me and the whole created order is being drawn. So, the company of heaven, the angels and the saints, is best understood as the beginning of our whole cosmos caught up in and woven through by the life of God. We see the joyfulness of this company of heaven in our first two Scripture passages today: from Revelations and from Psalm 34. Here is a vision of human beings at home with God and with all the deepest mysteries of the unseen world, rejoicing and free and all together.

In light of this vision, I think that Protestant objections to the prayers of the saints, and to our addressing prayers to them, seem unnecessary. Christ is the vine and the prayers of the saints are part of the sap, the lifeblood of that vine. Likewise, Christ is the sun, but Mary and all the saints shine with the beauty of the moon. The saints are inseparable from Christ, and Christ is the life of the saints. So, limiting our prayers to Christ only, also denying that the saints can pray for us, misses the whole glorious holism and mutuality of heaven. It misses the extent to which God's sovereign grace has *found its mark already in transformed human hearts*, that it *has* begun enfolding the world into God through the resurrection of Jesus Christ. Likewise, to say that the prayers of the saints for us are unnecessary seems to me to be the counsel of spoilsports. God isn't a thin-lipped Protestant accountant, fixated on the bottom line. God's more like a flamboyant Italian impresario who simply won't keep to budget!

So how can the saints who love us not be seen to pray for us, if it's true that their hearts and God's heart now beat as one? If prayer for someone means loving them consciously before God, then our continuing love for the blessed dead and their continuing love for us, likewise the saints' intercession for us and our invocation of their help, all fit together in the exuberant, joyfully expanding reality which is the life of God the Holy Trinity. It's into that life that our lives are being drawn *this very day* through word and sacrament, lifting up our hearts to that place where, with all the saints and angels, we hope one day to be revealed as we truly are.

The Lord be with you....

All Saints' Day, and just in time ...

All Saints' Day, 1 November 2020, Year A,
St Philip's, O'Connor

Revelation 7:9-17; Psalm 34:1-10, 22; 1 John 3:1-3; Matthew 5:1-12

† In the Name of the Father and of the Son and of the Holy Spirit. Amen.

In *The New York Review of Books* this week, the American essayist, playwright and actor Wallace Shawn cast his mind back over seventy years and asked how things had changed in his country. It's not that America was ever as pure and righteous as it likes to think, he concluded; it's just that now, people have stopped pretending. His comments refer to the Gospel passage for this All Saints' Day, from Jesus' Sermon on the Mount, so I'm going to quote him at length. Here's some of what Wallace Shawn had to say.

> Trump has liberated a lot of people from the last vestiges of the Sermon on the Mount. A lot of people turn out to have been sick and tired of pretending to be good. The fact that the leader of one of our two parties – the party, in fact, that has for many decades represented what was normal, acceptable, and respectable – was not ashamed to reveal his own selfishness, was not ashamed to reveal his own indifference to the suffering of others, was not even ashamed to reveal his own cheerful enjoyment of cruelty ... all of this helped people to feel that they no longer needed to be ashamed of those qualities in themselves either. They didn't need to feel bad because they didn't care about other people. Maybe they didn't want to be forbearing toward enemies. Maybe they didn't want to be gentle or kind.
>
> In a world in which the rich want permission to take as much as they can get without feeling any shame, and many of

the not-rich are so worried about their own sinking fortunes that they find it hard to worry about the misery of anyone else, Trump is the priest who grants absolution. In a way, he seems to be telling his followers that perhaps compassion is just one more value of the elite culture that he and they hate, like speaking in long sentences and listening to classical music.[15]

So says Wallace Shawn. Now, it's a sobering fact that many conservative Christians in America, both Catholic and Protestant, share in this new culture of weaponised grievance, contempt and spitefulness. Jesus' vision in today's Gospel is notably absent when no credit is being given to meekness or mercy or peacemaking, while perverse, self-justifying versions of purity and righteousness are gaining ground.

Jesus knew what his saints would have to face. He tells us in today's Gospel that the saints are going to be persecuted and spoken evil of because they refuse to play by the familiar rules. Likewise, our Revelations reading identifies the blessed in heaven as those who've come out of a great ordeal. And here's why the lamb is such a powerful symbol in that reading. Paradoxically, this mildest of creatures, and everywhere slain, is now the central Christian image of Jesus' own triumph and that of his saints because it's a triumph of mercy and peace, not of violence and wrathful payback. William Blake distinguished the lamb from a fierce predator in his great poem "The Tyger", but here it's the lamb of God that we see burning bright in the forest of the night, with a fearful symmetry spelling not predation but salvation, not death but life.

Friends, Jesus' teaching in our Gospel today isn't best understood as *prescriptive*, telling us what to do but, rather, as *descriptive*, telling us what the saints are and have always been doing – and why, and how. Because this alternative, paradoxical triumph of love in the midst of death and defeat *is* playing out in history;

---

15 Wallace Shawn, "Developments Since My Birth", *The New York Review of Books* 27 October 2020.

All Saints' Day

because God *is* crafting a miracle of genuine, life-giving purity and righteousness from the warped timber of actual human existence. Today's Gospel isn't an *aspiration*, then, it's an *observation*! And what we observe is God's craftsmanship at work in ordinary lives, even yours and mine.

The temptation of course is to distance ourselves from the saints, perhaps to put them on a pedestal, contenting ourselves with a few half-hearted gestures in the direction of holiness. But today's Epistle from 1 John makes clear that sanctity is not alien; that you and I are among the saints already, in the sense of being God's children *now*, and on a journey to becoming something that we can't imagine. Instead of a half-lived Christian life, then, which is all that many Christians aspire to, the final revelation of our identity is imagined here as oneness with God, so that in the meantime we have every reason to purify ourselves as God is pure – to start living out our truest destiny here and now.

Fr Martin properly warned us last week about the dangers of purity – purity of the wrong sort, that is – so here I commend Søren Kierkegaard's reliable definition: purity of heart is to will one thing. Now, this doesn't mean that there's only one way to be a saint. There are many ways, as our Revelation reading today imagines it: a heaven of diverse, multinational, multilingual, transhistorical humanity, faithful no doubt in so many ways, having answered the demands and lived under the conditions of many different ages. A favourite All Saints' hymn captures this diversity of ways in which the saints exhibit this single purity:

> Some march with events to turn them God's way.
> Some need to withdraw, the better to pray.
> Some carry the Gospel through fire and through flood –
> the world is their parish; their purpose is God.[16]

---

16 "Rejoice in God's Saints", in *Together in Song: Australian Hymn Book II* (Melbourne: HarperCollins*Religious*, 1999), #470 (sung to the tune *Paderborn*).

There's a glory in this that's meant to lift up our hearts. And here in the Eucharist that lifting up of our hearts is meant to take place – lifted up into God's holiness; lifted beyond the world of ugly self-assertion, contempt and hatred that batters on the doors of our imagination. Instead, here today we participate in the vision of our Revelation reading, which imagines heaven as a great Eucharistic celebration, with martyred saints and angels and other heavenly powers gathered around the throne and the lamb of God just as a company of the early Church's newly baptised would have gathered around their bishop, robed in white, for the Easter Eucharist.

So, I invite you to compare what we're doing here today with a Trump rally – with its celebration of vindictiveness and contempt; with the fleeting relief it offers from an eroded self-image. Christians can do better than that, and with that in mind it helps us to remember that we belong among God's saints *already*, straining upwards with them in the high calling of humility, mercy and peacemaking; welcomed into a purity and righteousness that doesn't have to be asserted at others' expense. Because the world needs its saints – it needs them to step up, and now! Otherwise the alternative is just too awful.

The Lord be with you ...

Christ the King
(The Reign of Christ)

Faith and Relevance

Christ the King, 26 November 2006, Year B,
St Christopher's Catholic Cathedral, Manuka

Daniel 7:13-14; Revelation 1:5-8; John 18:33-37

† In the Name of the Father and of the Son and of the Holy Spirit. Amen.

Once I went with a friend to one of Australia's great Protestant churches, and heard a preacher, reputed to be one of Australia's best. There were hundreds of people there. My excited friend said that people went to this church because the sermons were so *relevant*, so helpful for people trying to live their lives. On this particular occasion, the minister spoke about the importance of companionship, and a very interesting talk it was. My friend was much helped by it, she said, because she was in the middle of deciding whether or not to relocate interstate and was weighing up moving away from her friends against other factors. She seemed to be saying that this sort of practical wisdom was what preaching ought to offer. When I pointed out that there was nothing about God in the sermon – nothing about the Gospel of Jesus Christ, nothing about a new way of being, of forgiveness, of a new creation, nothing about a vision to give a whole new perspective on life – she looked at me blankly, as people often look at theologians blankly.

A parishioner has occasionally looked at me blankly, too. One dear lady in my first parish, in Brisbane, gently told me that she never really understood my sermons, no matter how hard she tried. I probed this a little, and found it had nothing to do with long words, or with complicated reasoning, which I was pleased to hear, as I try to be clear and straightforward. No, it was more to do with the whole point of preaching. She expected, and I think a lot of people expect, that sermons will be interesting, informative talks, ideally with some entertainment thrown in, some diversion, rather like those so-called Infotainment programs and all those cooking shows. The sermon should be *relevant*, it should be a help for us in our lives, not telling us things we don't need to know, not telling us things we don't want to hear. Many don't want to know how the Sunday Gospel and other readings might best be understood, for instance; and many don't want to hear sustained reflection on life in light of the Gospel, reflection which opens us up to new insights and challenges. I suspect that many of us prefer preaching that fits into our lives, and a religion that's comforting, not challenging.

And here I think many Anglicans, many Christians in general, are like Pontius Pilate in today's Gospel. Pontius Pilate is trying to interpret Jesus according to his own categories, isn't he, with his questions? He's quizzing Jesus, to see if Jesus fitted into the world he knew: "Are you a king?", he asks. In the same way, some of us put Jesus on trial, and put the Christian faith on trial, to see if it fits in with our priorities, with the world as we see it. But instead of asking "are you a king?", our question is "are you relevant to my life, are you relevant to my existing priorities in life?"

But apart from all such questions of *relevance*, Jesus raises the uncomfortable question of the *truth* in today's gospel, boldly stating that all who love and serve the truth will come to him. In other words, it's not about the relevance of Christianity to our lives; it's not about fitting Jesus and God and the Church into our lives, or not, or only the bits we like. Rather, it's exactly the opposite. It's about fitting our lives, our dreams, our priorities into God's life, into Jesus' life. It's about learning from the God of Jesus Christ what's important, what's worthwhile, and putting that first in our lives. It's about being caught up in the life of God, rather than God being given a place in our lives. We see this happening in today's Gospel where Jesus is put on trial by Pilate, but ends up putting Pilate on trial, with Jesus putting questions to Pilate rather than the other way around.

So, it is for us in our Eucharist today, when we dare to name Jesus Christ as King – King of the Universe, King of love, King of hearts. The question isn't "how is this relevant to my life?"; the question is, "how is my life relevant to what God is doing in the world?"; the question is, "how does my life, how do my priorities, fit in with the life and the priorities of the Kingdom of God?" Does all of this religious practice have to serve me, and make me feel better, surer, more comfortable? Or is this Eucharist, week by week, about *responding to God's initiative*, is it about opening our hearts to be softened, about opening our minds to be changed, about opening our wills to be galvanised, about allowing our lives to be caught up in God's purposes?

Our reading from Daniel imagines a world where God's peace and God's sanity and God's good will find a human face. Our reading from the Apocalypse calls the whole world to account before the challenge of Jesus Christ, so that those who oppose him and sell him short are well and truly put on notice.

Instead of a superficial relevance, instead of an easy message, instead of a little boost to help us on our way, God takes us and our purpose in life altogether more seriously. For us, gathered at this altar, there's nothing less than the assurance of a new identity, of a mission in life, of a purpose for living that burns hotter and carries farther than any superficial relevance. The Feast of Christ the King is about nothing less than being caught up in God's life. This is the relevance that God offers you and me in word and sacrament.

The Lord be with you...

Sovereignty Beyond Monarchy and Republic

Christ the King, 21 November 2010, Year C,
St Saviour's Anglican Cathedral, Goulburn

Jeremiah 23:1-6; The Benedictus; Colossians 1:11-20; Luke 23:33-43

✝ In the Name of the Father and of the Son and of the Holy Spirit. Amen.

This last Sunday of the Church's annual calendar is devoted to Christ the King, and just when we might think that ideas of kingship are impossibly old-fashioned and irrelevant to our lives today, the media and the internet are full of news about a royal wedding. Prince William and Kate Middleton are to marry – King William V and Queen Catherine in waiting. The issue of kings and queens has been much debated in Australia: are we better off with the constitutional monarchy, with sovereignty vested in the King or Queen, or are the republicans right that sovereignty properly belongs to the people? Which model is better at doing what sovereignty is meant to do: ensuring justice, maintaining law and order, creating the opportunity for peace and prosperity?

Some say that monarchy and the social hierarchy it presupposes keeps us respectful, which makes for a more just and peaceful society. Others say that equality before the law isn't enough, and that a republican model ensures true equality. Of course, the world's oldest stable republic, the American one, with its strange mix of equality and inequality, with its culture of envy, rivalry and extraordinary levels of violence, might make us wonder whether vesting sovereignty in the people alone really does make for a more rather than less just and peaceful society. Whichever way we ultimately go, the fact of sovereignty, the power of the state – its legal claim over the individual, the rule of law, the state's monopoly on violence within its borders through the armed forces, the police and the penal system – reminds us that we humans need looking after and protecting from ourselves.

The Christian tradition, following on from Israel's story in the Old Testament, believes that stability and order in society is something God endorses, blessing lawful sovereignty in the nations of our world for the sake of human well-being. In other words, the state, the king, or the president, the parliament and the law courts, the military and the police, are all signs of God's tough love.

But the clue to really understanding this is to realise that God's sovereignty, which stands above every claim for national sovereignty, is exercised for the sake of our human family that God loves and cares for. British sovereigns are crowned by the Church for this reason, and parliamentary sessions commence with prayer. Like it or not in our secular and multi-faith society, these traditions are a reminder that the nation's claims are not absolute, that its sovereign authority is limited, that the King is God's servant.

Our first reading, from the prophet Jeremiah, makes this very clear, declaring God's disappointment over bad and corrupt leaders in the nation, who have failed to shepherd God's people justly. Instead of a Psalm today, we had the Benedictus, the song of Zechariah anticipating the birth of John the Baptist, and a new day when God would renew the Kingship in Israel – when God would bring a new shepherd to God's people, of whom John the Baptist would be witness. Here the prayer of God's people for a good king, like King David in the old days, expresses a longing not just for order and stability in society, but for a new future in which the deep unfulfilled longings of human hearts would be fulfilled. And this is precisely what God gives us in the one whom John the Baptist proclaims, Jesus Christ.

In Jesus, we get the promised King, but not as many expected. Those who dreamed of kicking the Romans out so that Israel becomes a great nation again were to be disappointed. Jesus was not that sort of King. And those who look to the Church as a safe and non-threatening organ of society are going to be disappointed too: those who look to us for respectability, prudential morality, and conventional values – the kinds of things many people say that they're seeking when they bring their children for baptism, for instance, or send them to a church school. I'm afraid Jesus is always likely to disappoint these people, because he isn't respectable, because he doesn't fit in with normal priorities and conventional wisdom, because he demonstrates that preserving the status quo can never be the whole story with God. In other words, in Jesus Christ, God shows his more adventurous side. In Jesus Christ, God takes off humanity's training wheels, calling us to adventures with God beyond social stability, beyond the conventional values which, of course, matter to God but which can never be the whole story. Christ the King is a different sort of King. And today's Gospel shows just how different he is.

Christ the King appears in today's Gospel as a condemned criminal and the friend of condemned criminals. No respectable position in society here, to which our Anglican Church used to be so wedded in Australia – with our white gloves in church and nice cups of tea with nice people after, and all very proper. In jarring contrast to all this, Jesus is condemned to death as a rebel by the Roman Empire. Why? Because he dared to remind Rome who the real God was – that Caesar had overstepped himself, like sovereign authorities before and since have overstepped themselves, building peace and stability ultimately at the cost of much injustice, violence and suffering. Jesus forgives those who crucify him in today's Gospel, but in so doing he declares the sovereign authority that condemned him to be in the wrong and denies that it has any proper power over him. He judges it, not the other way around – though on this occasion he chooses to forgive. And as for the criminal alongside him with enough wit to shake off the mob mentality and see Jesus for who he really is, the death sentence of Rome is overridden: "today you will be with me in Paradise".

In our Epistle reading from Colossians, the extent of Jesus' differentness is explained. This crucified one whose death everyone agreed on – except the friendly thief on the cross, that is – reveals how things really are with God. In Jesus crucified we see God's patient, self-involving struggle to change things in our world, with injustice and cruelty shown up and disempowered, with deviated power structures called back to a proper attitude of reserve and of service to others – forgiving our sins, like he forgave the thief on the cross; rescuing us from the darkness of business as usual in human history to discover something new.

We hear in this Colossians passage that Jesus Christ is our clue to understanding the whole creation, so that all the powers of this world – thrones, dominions, principalities – find their proper level only with reference to who he is and what he does. All things ultimately hold together in him – in his sacrificial love and mercy revealing what God is persistently up to in our world. This is in stark contrast with the Empires, the ideologies, the markets, and all the other secondary realities that are meant to serve human good, but which end up thinking that they're God. Jesus' cross stands at the turning point of human history, judging and revealing all other versions of human greatness, of human leadership, of human order, of human stability. It reveals the reality of our sinful world, where sovereignty in society regularly lets us down; yet it also reveals the loving heart of God, who subverts and transforms things from within – a God who won't be annexed to the status quo as its ultimate guarantor and preserver. Christ the King isn't against Kings, or Presidents for that matter. But he is God with us, God for us, supporting the structures of our world where they serve God's justice and compassion, but exposing them and undermining them and hastening their end when they lose the plot.

In this reality of Jesus Christ, the Church finds its identity and calling, as our Colossians reading concludes today. The Church of the crucified Jesus, the Church whose Lord was universally condemned as a rebel and as a disgrace to religion, is a risky bet if we're looking for the respectable and the conventional. Our baptism isn't a mark of conventionality and respectability as much as our enlistment in an adventure, and who knows where we'll end up in Jesus' company? Christ the King, who claims us in baptism, who reclaims us with love with every Eucharist, points beyond the powers that be in this world, and all its conventional prudential wisdom, to where our deepest loyalty, our truest identity and our ultimate obedience lie.

The Lord be with you...

Christmas (Midnight Mass)

What Sort of Lord do we Meet in the Christmas Gospel?

Midnight Mass of Christmas, 2003,
St Paul's, Manuka

Isaiah 9:2-7; Psalm 96; Titus 2:11-14; Luke 2:1-14

✝ In the Name of the Father and of the Son and of the Holy Spirit. Amen.

When Lisa and I were travelling in Eastern Europe some years ago, we visited a great Roman Catholic sacred site – the Shrine of the Infant of Prague. The infant is a little wax statue of the Christ child, about 400 years old now, who sits in a glass case on a side altar in a Church belonging to the Carmelite Friars – an exquisite but fragile doll about so high. And they dress him up, like a million Barbies will be dressed up which on this Christmas Eve eagerly wait in their gift-wrapping for tomorrow morning's urgent little hands. The Infant has numerous regal outfits, in the various church colours. He's got a little orb and sceptre, too – the Infant of Prague presents the Christ child to us as Lord of the world. I mention all of this as a way in for us to the theme of Christmas, to help us answer the question, "what sort of Lord do we meet in the Christmas gospel"?

There are stories about the Infant of Prague: that he's a miracle-working statue, who over the centuries has spoken to priests in their prayers. The fortunes of the Prague Carmelites have risen and fallen, so the story goes, according to the honour they've given to the statue. The Infant even survived the sack of Prague and desecration of his Church in the 17th century, when he was rescued from a rubbish tip after several years. Today these miracle stories are alive and well.

We went to two Masses at the shrine during our visit to Prague. At the first mass there was an American priest who had brought a tour group of Filipino women on a pilgrimage. He preached to them about the miracle-working power of the statue, and one after another these poor women drew close, and knelt, and poured out God knows what woes, God knows what bitter stories as wives, as mothers, as people ground down by harsh circumstance. And I couldn't help thinking that religion was there, its God was there, performing its long-accustomed task: serving as an aid to denial, as a reassuring escapism to help struggling individuals cope with the bitterness of life. The little King, gloriously arrayed, would magically save them. And religion will make their life bearable, as a smooth veil of comfort drawn over the stark reality of existence. The Marxists who'd run things in Prague not long before we were there would have recognised this religion all too well: Marx famously called it the soul of soulless conditions, the opium of the people.

I remember feeling angry during this sermon. It seemed to betray that fragile little infant statue, and the truth he could tell us if we listened, and the religion he could commend to us – a religion that might have an answer for Marx, for his critique of religion and for modern atheism more generally. Let me tell you what I mean.

Often, religion descends into sentimentality and escapism. We see this in the cult of the Infant of Prague, in the sort of religious belief that's magical and irrational, that delights to fly in the face of experience. Many people reject religion, thinking it's all like this, and I'd have to say that their instincts in rejecting superstition are good.

Others don't reject religion; they just ignore it. But abandoning religion doesn't mean abandoning escapism. There's much secular escapism, too. We numb ourselves with our various addictions, mild or serious; we divert ourselves constantly, with workaholism or sport or net surfing or sex or shopping; we cheat frailty and death with diet or exercise or plastic surgery, and by hiding away from us out of sight the mad, the grossly deformed, the frail elderly; we pin our hopes on our children; we follow leaders or gurus be they political, psychological, financial or spiritual, and we think they'll save us from emptiness. Or, if we're talented and creative, we may try to create our own version of the world, our own meaning, as artists and thinkers have always done – though this is so demanding a task that many give way under it, hence the close connection between creativity and madness.

Because, if we can't mask the terror of life and death, madness awaits, even suicide. This is why suicide is on the rise, especially for the young, and especially at Christmas. Because we've lost the belief system that once knit our social life together, haven't we? The 'Snakes and Ladders' game is no longer given as a Christmas present, I suspect, because who could believe its just and reassuring version of things any more, at a time when pride doesn't come before a fall, but before a bigger parcel of stock options, and when diligence leads not to promotion but to redundancy. At a time when yesterday's heroism is dissolved in today's cynicism; when yesterday's dogged faith gives way to today's plural confusion.

But it needn't be like this, and here the Christmas Gospel can help us see something different – a different sort of God, and a different kind of religion. Let me tell you about the other Mass we went to at the shrine in Prague. There was a passionate young Carmelite Friar preaching when we came in, in Czech, and we couldn't understand a word. But then he started pointing to the statue of the infant and drawing comparisons. I heard him saying something that sounded to me like "Jesu Christi/Communisti", "Jesu Christi/Mafiosi". I understood that he was comparing the vision of Christ with alternatives that had so threatened and undermined his country – the Soviet communism which crushed the Prague Spring of 1968, sweeping away its "communism with a human face", along with the gangster capitalism now ruling the roost throughout Eastern Europe since the cold war. Against these resolute forces of denial – fiercely ideological communism and heartless human greed – the young friar seemed to be pointing to an alternative, hinted at by this frail and tiny statue. It was a great sermon, even though I understood only a few words of it!

As the young Czech priest spoke, it struck me that the power of the Infant of Prague isn't in his alleged miracle-working ability. Rather, it's in his very frailty, it's in his very waxen ordinariness, which is so like the ordinariness, so like the fragility of our own threatened flesh. I couldn't help thinking that this is how God meets us in the real world – not as an ideology of denial, but as a human infant, as one of us, in all the compromised, threatened, limited earthiness and ordinariness and frankness of our embodied lives.

The infant of Christmas is God's answer for frail and fearful human beings, burdened with a spiritual vocation which somehow we have to work out. Though we have to do so as fragile bodies every bit as tenuous as the wax body of that statue. But this takes us to the heart of the Christmas Gospel, and the Good Friday Gospel for that matter: that God meets us and embraces our condition from within it, not from above it, not by denying it. And this is the hardest spiritual lesson of life for us to learn, when even if we're religious we so often miss the point, replacing ordinary secular escapism and denial with religious escapism and denial. Instead, as Martin Luther said, the power of God is nowhere more evident than in the manger and on the cross.

God doesn't force us to make our own meaning and leave most of us to lives of denial and escapism because that's the best we can do. Rather, God patiently offers us God's very self under the limited, time-bound conditions of our lives. And as one of us, God transforms our lives and our deaths. Thus, the sacraments, thus the Church, thus the rituals we celebrate Sunday by Sunday in places like this, where we're invited to re-imagine our lives in terms of Immanuel, God with us. God's Christmas gift to us is seen in the waxen frailty of the Infant of Prague, in the fleshly frailty of the Infant of Bethlehem. And it's seen in the dogged, realistic hope and patience and virtue that God can call forth even from us, even from you and me, whom God sets free to live open-eyed lives, beyond denial and escapism.

The Lord be with you...

Joyeux Nöel

Midnight Mass of Christmas, 2005,
St Paul's, Manuka

Isaiah 9:2-7; Psalm 96: Titus 2:11-14; Luke 2:1-14

✝ In the Name of the Father and of the Son and of the Holy Spirit. Amen.

Have you been to the arthouse cinema of late to see *Joyeux Nöel*, the new pan-European movie about the extraordinary Christmas Truce of 1914? If not, you must fit it in between *King Kong* and *The Lion, the Witch and the Wardrobe* in your post-Christmas movie going.

Here and there, throughout Northern France in the first year of World War I, when the conflict hadn't sunk into year in, year out relentless bitterness and before towns and forests began to disappear into a featureless, reeking quagmire, something extraordinary and spontaneous happened on Christmas Eve. Peace broke out, carols were sung, food parcels from home and grog and laughter were shared in no-man's land, and on Christmas day, the dead were buried, soccer games were played and the war that had divided Europe gave way to the ancient Christian faith that united it, if only for a couple of days.

Before long, the top brass insisted on a return to hostilities, and not always sensitively, with punishment for some officers who'd broken ranks and joined the unofficial truce. For me, whether or not we believe all the Christmas Bible stories about virgins and stars and wise men, the real miracle of Christmas emerges again and again through history as the Prince of Peace works his liberating magic in human hearts, displacing the narrower, more predictable divinities that we humans regularly prefer.

Christmas (Midnight Mass)

In *Joyeux Nöel*, it's German and French and Scottish troops who meet in a Christmas truce. The key players are the German opera singer turned foot soldier whose lovely rendering of *Stille Nacht, Heilige Nacht* drifts across to the allied trenches, and the Scottish priest Palmer, who joins in the tune on his bagpipes, then leads in 'O Come All Ye Faithful', which the German singer takes up in Latin, venturing into no-man's land with a candle-lit Christmas tree held aloft instead of a white flag.

Later that night, Palmer celebrates the Eucharist in no-man's land and the bitter enemies are united in praise of the Christ child, who relativises and stills all their enmities. As Father Palmer reflects afterwards, "those men were drawn to that altar as if it was a warm fire on a winter's night", perhaps a little like you and me who are drawn here tonight, unsure perhaps of what we make of all this, but quite certain that there has to be more in store for human beings than a world ruled by dehumanising forces: by violence, by blinkered ideology, by blind fate and by the false gods that human cultures perennially manufacture, projecting their own defining biases and hatreds and making idols of them.

All this we see in the middle East, as the Iraqi factions circle uneasily around an elusive peace, or as our American friends struggle to keep their values intact in the face of war's many temptations, or in the southern beaches of our own major city, right here in supposedly tolerant Australia, where the clash of civilisations is being played out between white and Lebanese Australians – also the clash of winners and losers in the global economy, which we saw most recently on the streets of France, and before that in the aftermath of Hurricane Katrina. This is what we humans are like, and we make idols of our differences, keeping order by making scapegoats against whom everyone can join in venting their anger. This is typical human religion, at work even in supposedly secular societies. It was there in the war depicted in *Joyeux Nöel*, with tribal gods very much in the ascendant – *Gott mit Uns*, God with us, wasn't the slogan just of the Germans, but of every side in the conflict, with everyone's righteous cause prosecuted against the demonised other.

But the religion of Christmas is the reverse of all the business as usual religion that humanity unfailingly generates. And we see this in our readings tonight. Isaiah the prophet has had enough of war and defeat, and dreams of the day when "all the boots of the tramping warriors and all the garments rolled in blood shall be burned as fuel for the fire", because "a child has been born for us, a son given to us... and he is named Wonderful Counsellor, Mighty God, Everlasting Father, Prince of Peace". The authority that rests on the shoulders of this mighty one was evident in the Christmas Truce of 1914, when the false gods of proud human self-definition yielded to the real God, whose indelible mark is universal peace and brotherhood. This is the God of the nations, of whom our Psalmist sings tonight – not just of one nation at the expense of another, but of all nations who find they don't need an enemy and a scapegoat to make a meaningful human world. Somehow, this fragile child who grew up and dies on a cross carried a power from God able to unite us more powerfully than the false gods to which we cling have the power to divide.

This is controversial news, this Christmas Gospel, and it can't help but be political. It's a mistake to be sentimental and otherworldly when we seek the deepest meaning of Christmas. Rather, it's a reality that presents itself on battlefields awash with blood, and it's the judgment of every human pretension. Why else would Luke have given us that extraordinary tongue-in-cheek Gospel we heard tonight, so subversive of the Roman Empire and its pretensions. Tonight's Gospel begins in the realm of the divine Caesar Augustus, his Governor Quirinius and his Empire, and the census he took as a sign of his dominion over the whole world, and where is the action? It's not in their realm, not in their plans and the organisation of their world-wide domination, but in a stable out the back of an inn, entirely outside their world and its priorities and its pomps. The witnesses to God's new thing were shepherds, who were homeless

Christmas (Midnight Mass)

vagabonds and social outsiders according to the wisdom of the day – ferals, gypsies.

This is the arena in which the true God is revealed, gently but firmly putting on notice all the false Gods of human invention, all our Empires, ideologies and self-justifying pretensions. Instead, "Glory to God in the highest heaven, and on earth peace".

This is the God in whose name we gather tonight, and in our reading from the letter to Titus we hear the sort of attitude that befits the people of the real God – a God "training us to renounce impiety and worldly passions, and in the present age to live lives that are self-controlled, upright and Godly, while we wait for the blessed hope and the manifestation of the glory of our great God and Saviour, Jesus Christ". Too much unhelpful Christian teaching down the centuries has made us think about sex when we hear these words, as if the message here is tight sexual self-restraint. In light of everything I've been saying, however, I hear this challenge from Titus as a challenge to live with restraint and humility in a world of overheated religious passions and ideological claims, not buying into the violent self-assertion that makes our normal human world go around, but keeping a cool and sober watchfulness over everything overblown and grandiose and remembering that the real sacred, the one who is not an idol, who is ever coming to meet and to claim us, relativises every human claim to absolute power and absolute truth.

At the end of *Joyeux Noël*, this is all put very plainly. The English bishop comes to the front to preach a Christmas sermon to the troops, exhorting them to kill with clear consciences because theirs is a holy war. The priest Palmer is chastised by the bishop and told he's being sent back to his parish in Scotland. His role in the Christmas truce has proved that he's no longer suitable to be a military chaplain; he no longer belongs with good Christian fighting men in the Lord's house. Father Palmer protests that his place is with the suffering and with those who've lost their faith, but the Bishop is unmoved – his eyes are on a different god, a tribal god.

We know that priests and bishops preached war as a Christian duty up and down the Empire, including in this country, just as other religious leaders today are preaching Jihad. And neither are preaching the real god, only tribal religion – different at one level, but underneath, anthropologically identical. No, Father Palmer and the German opera singer, and the soldiers who saw beyond their differences into the meaning of it all at Christmas, were in touch with the real God, and so are we here tonight – a God who is not against anybody, a God who is not the champion of one culture or religion against another, a God who wears the particular face of Jesus Christ, but who is betrayed if Jesus Christ is made into a slogan to attack anyone, to dehumanise anyone. Christmas is the ultimate critique of the human religious impulse, of all warmongering, all ethnic cleansing, of all anxious, selfish tribalism. When we look in love to the Christ child this Christmas, when we sing "O come let us adore him", it is at nobody's expense, and it is for everyone's good.

A happy Christmas to you all...

Christmas Day

The Word Became Flesh – Yes, *Flesh*

Christmas Day (second Mass of the day), 2011,
All Saints', Ainslie

Isaiah 52:7-10; Psalm 98:1-4; Hebrews 1:1-4; John 1:1-14

✝ In the Name of the Father and of the Son and of the Holy Spirit. Amen.

And the Word became flesh and lived among us, and we have seen his glory ... (John 1:14).

In this third, and last, of the Church's three Masses for Christmas day, our readings from the Bible focus on the meaning of Christ's coming. The beautiful words of Isaiah's prophecy announce to God's ancient people – to that long-suffering nation of asylum seekers and dreamers – that the God who always loved them and protected them was coming to rebuild ruined Jerusalem, to renew the people of God, to stick up for them once again before all their self-proclaimed betters among the nations. And all this was to happen in plain sight, as Isaiah declares – in plain socio-political history.

Our Psalm this morning is lovely: God's people then and now, in Israel and in the Church, can rejoice because a marvellous thing is coming from God. The letter to the Hebrews in our second reading explains how Jesus fulfils these promises in person, as "the reflection of God's glory and the exact imprint of God's very being". John's Gospel puts this insight in different language, talking today about God's Word becoming flesh. Friends, this is wonderful news. But it's strange news, too. It's not what people expect – not then; not now. This is why John's Gospel also tells us today that Jesus came to his own people and they didn't receive him. And they still don't want to know him, in large numbers, do they, up and down our Western world? Or, if they do want to know him, it's on their own terms, not his.

The problem we have is that this message of God coming to us in the flesh is confronting for us on two levels. It doesn't fit with how we prefer to understand God, and it doesn't fit with how we prefer to see ourselves.

Regarding our preferred understanding of God, we find this Christian message too specific, and perhaps too demanding. God's fine these days as some sort of metaphysical speculation. But, instead of some private opinion or spirituality of the heart, on Christmas day we're handed a squirming baby by God – *and* he's a baby who wants to take over our life, as babies do. Then, of course, this baby Jesus starts growing up, and asking awkward questions, and upsetting the way things normally go. In fact, he's such a pain that eventually he has to be judicially murdered to shut him up. But then his resurrection is revealed as God's great game changer, uprooting once and for all the fear and paralysis that makes for lives of docile predictability.

Rather than today's widespread preference for non-committal spirituality, then, which gives us some comfort and which we can more or less control, this squirming Christmas baby brings with him a whole extended family of fellow Christians who want us to be part of their lives. And, of course, babies come with a lot of paraphernalia, as every young parent knows – in Jesus' case it's Scripture and sacraments, it's Church and creed. Better to leave this squirming baby behind when we leave church today, don't you think – this Word become noisy and demanding flesh, with all his weird followers and all their strange expectations? Better to keep God safe in the realm of the spiritual, in the realm of take it or leave it, don't you think?

The other difficulty we have with the Word become flesh has to do with our own attitude to the flesh: that is, to actual human life. Being a creature of flesh means being limited in our options; it means belonging to our own time and, to some extent still, to our own place. It means having to work out our human life within a whole world of boundaries. We're creatures shaped by a particular language, ethnicity and gender; we're people with a particular life story that we can't entirely choose; we're physical bodies with particular needs, possibilities and limitations; we're creatures who belong to this particular family, to this particular spouse, to this particular set of commitments, to this particular occupation, to this particular home, and so it goes. All this is seen nowadays as an unbearable state of affairs by many people, in what the advertisers want us to believe is a new age of infinite choices. We hate to be tied down, to be subject to the predictable, to be denied the specialness and distinctiveness that we just *know* to be our right. Constraint and limitation, authority and custom, tradition and belonging, can barely be tolerated because, if we're settled and stable, we won't be the restless consumers that a growth economy needs us to be.

These days, with texting, tweeting and social networking recasting what relationships look like, the flesh becomes a liability, the face-to-face becomes an unnecessary and unwelcome extra, the long-term commitment becomes increasingly unthinkable and unendurable – or, at the very least, it becomes optional. Apparently, we're more comfortable as nodes in an electronic network than as creatures of flesh, embedded in particular communities and relationships. To an extent, we even punish our flesh. Unfit, overweight people like me take risks with our health, because in one way or another we resist the wisdom of our bodies, of our definite physical nature, which calls on us to be more active and to eat simply and well. Yet the lean, sexy and networked also punish their flesh, with savage exercise regimes, piercing, tattooing, utilitarian sexuality, drug use, and smoking to help stay thin.

But life in the flesh is also life in the physical environment where all living creatures belong, and here we're just as uncomfortable with the limitations placed upon us. Increasingly, as a civilization, we're resisting the increasingly urgent call to live sustainably in our physical world. We refuse the evidence of just how serious climate change is, because, if we accepted it, we'd have to adapt to the actual conditions of our physical world, of our flesh – we'd have to become people of serious sober restraint in how we inhabit our world. And who wants that?

One more thing. We also resent the increasing complexity of life in our world, with many people running away from it in the grip of anxiety. Yet in our postmodern era we have to face the fact that pluralism is here to stay. Coping positively with the diversity of people and lifestyles is what life in the real world is going to require from now on, and that's just that – though not for an increasing number of anxious and embittered individuals and movements. The God whose Word became flesh doesn't deplore this state of affairs but, plainly, many people do. They prefer fantasy worlds of nostalgic purity, uncomplicated authority, and over-simple choices. Yet the simple truth for us creatures of flesh is that there's only one world where we can make a go of it, and that's *this* world – with all its complexities, frustrations, and in-your-face diversity.

So, what does it mean for us today that the Word became flesh and lived among us, and that we have seen his glory? It means that this squirming baby Jesus of Christmas brings God to us with a shocking new realism, also confirming us in a shocking new earthiness and groundedness as human beings. God comes to transform our lives in the real world. It means that rather than escapists to heaven, we're called to share God's investment in healing the earth. It means that rather than fantasists with our heads in the clouds, we're called to be committed people with our feet on the ground. It means that God calls us to dwell with peace and confidence in the midst of all this constraint and complexity, by not punishing our bodies, not resenting our particular commitments, not fearing the plurality of life. It means not avoiding the Church but accepting it as inevitable and appropriate; it means not preferring our own version of spirituality, but welcoming God's preference for sacramental earthiness.

Friends, today we get handed the squirming baby Jesus, and don't count on that old furphy about "no crying he makes". Jesus the Word of God comes in person to reveal God's glory in the flesh of this, the real world – the world God loves, and won't give up on.

The Lord be with you...

Joy of Heaven to Earth Come Down

Christmas Day (second Mass of the day), 2013,
All Saints', Ainslie

Isaiah 52:7-10; Psalm 98; Hebrews 1:1-4; John 1:1-14

† In the Name of the Father and of the Son and of the Holy Spirit. Amen.

The joy of Christmas means more than just a family celebration, a break from work, a chance to relax the diet, or a few luxurious days in front of the Boxing Day Test Match. It's all of these things, of course, but it points to something deeper. The Eucharist we celebrate and the Scripture readings we hear today point to the joy of God in our celebration – a joy that God is bursting to share with human beings.

Christmas joy is as old as creation, as our Hebrews reading tells us this morning. God creates and loves the world. Jesus Christ is the key to that creation, and the face of that love, to be found at the heart of what our world means. Jesus Christ is testified to here in this Hebrews passage as the exact imprint of God's being, and as the word that God has been insinuating into humanoid imaginations from prehistoric times – a word that has eventually taken visible shape and concrete form in the life of Jesus Christ. Our Hebrews reading pictures Jesus Christ as the pinnacle of creation, above the angels, and as the underlying theme of human history, sensed by the prophets of every age. Christmas celebrates the making flesh of this constant word, this constant love, this constant purpose, this constant presence of God. The joy of our Psalm this morning, with its trumpets and horns, is entirely fitting. Isaiah's invitation in our first reading – that the holy city should break into song – is what we're doing this morning with our carols. Our God remains a going concern; and Jesus is the missing piece that suddenly turns up in life to help us see life's puzzle whole and entire, perhaps for the first time, and to begin working things out in our lives – again, perhaps for the first time.

This is the promise of our gospel reading this morning, from the prologue of John, about the word becoming flesh. *Flesh*, of course, means human, it means real, it means vulnerable, it means here and now. And as for *word*: the Word of God stands at the centre of reality, and at the heart of life's meaning. So, instead of a philosophical principle or a vaporous spiritual something or other, the Word of God becomes a human life, and a historical project, and, among us today, the word of God becomes a sacramental presence given into our palms or placed on our tongue, as well as a spiritual gift for our imaginations.

This invitation is also a challenge. It was a challenge for Jesus himself when he came to his own people but they refused to know him, as we hear in our Gospel today. We human beings in general, and even many Christians, prefer a different word. We don't really welcome the silent, gentle approach of the Word made flesh. We prefer a more strident word, a more certain word, a more controlling word, often a more violent word.

There are many grim ideologies and utopian delusions that have galvanised human beings in the past, and still today, regardless of their cost. We'll build our view of the world on anything from America's social media-fuelled extremes of authoritarian populism, to Russia's pathetically grandiose empire building in Ukraine, or else we'll cling to fever dreams of unending economic growth while we refuse to take climate change seriously. We'd prefer any word as long as it isn't the word made flesh, and any option rather than taking life on God's terms. All of us reject God's invitation some of the time, while some reject it all of the time.

But, friends, God's joy and patience are unstoppable. And so, God's invitation comes back to us Christmas by Christmas, Easter by Easter and, of course, Sunday by Sunday as well. Whatever you may think life's about, here today it's about a robust joy that goes to the heart of our cosmos, to the root meaning of human history, and to the rusty levers that work the innermost dynamics of our own lives, to free them up and get them moving again.

The Lord be with you ...

Appendix

The Easter Anthems/Hymn to the Risen Christ

Alleluia.
Christ our Passover has been sacrificed for us;
therefore let us keep the feast,

Not with the old leaven, the leaven of malice and evil,
but with the unleavened bread of sincerity and truth. Alleluia.

Christ being raised from the dead will never die again;
death no longer has dominion over him.

The death that he died, he died to sin, once for all;
but the life he lives, he lives to God.

So also consider yourselves dead to sin,
and alive to God in Jesus Christ our Lord. Alleluia.

Christ has been raised from the dead,
the first fruits of those who have fallen asleep.

For since by a man came death,
by a man has come also the resurrection of the dead.

For as in Adam all die,
so also in Christ shall all be made alive. Alleluia.